MASTER THE ELECTRIC PRESSURE COOKER

MORE THAN 100 DELICIOUS RECIPES FROM BREAKFAST TO DESSERT

MARCI BUTTARS

Writer

Recipe Creator

Owner of the blog tidbits-marci.com

CAMI GRAHAM

Photographer

Interior Designer

Creator of TIDBITS, owner of the blog tidbits-cami.com

Skyhorse Publishing

Skyhorse Publishing books may be purchased in bulk at special discounts for sales promotion, corporate gifts, fund-raising, or educational purposes. Special editions can also be created to specifications. For details, contact the Special Sales Department, Skyhorse Publishing, 307 West 36th Street, 11th Floor, New York, NY 10018 or info@skyhorsepublishing.com.

Skyhorse® and Skyhorse Publishing® are registered trademarks of Skyhorse Publishing, Inc.®, a Delaware corporation.

Visit our website at www.skyhorsepublishing.com.

10 9 8 7 6 5 4 3 2 1

Names: Graham, Cami, author. | Buttars, Marci, author.
Title: Master the electric pressure cooker: more than 100 delicious recipes from breakfast to dessert / Cami Graham, Marci Buttars.
Description: New York, New York: Skyhorse Publishing, [2017]
Identifiers: LCCN 2017017313 | ISBN 9781680993004 (hardcover: alk. paper)
Subjects: LCSH: Pressure cooking. | Electric cooking. | LCGFT: Cookbooks.
Classification: LCC TX840.P7 G73 2017 | DDC 641.5/87—dc23 LC record available at https://lccn.loc.gov/2017017313

Cover design by Jane Sheppard
Cover photo by Cami Graham

Print ISBN: 978-1-68099-300-4

Printed in China

TABLE OF CONTENTS

ABOUT THE CREATORS

Marci is the mother of one sweet little girl and two high-energy twin boys. She's married to her motorcycle dream man, and together they are raising their family in a small town in Utah. She obtained a master's degree in nursing from Graceland University and currently works as a family nurse practitioner with an emphasis in pediatrics. She has a passion for health and wellness and enjoys teaching these skills to others. She also has a great excitement for cooking and enjoys experimenting with a variety of ingredients and ethnic foods. She is thrilled to be sharing these recipes in her first cookbook and alongside her sister Cami on *TIDBITS*. Other hobbies include motorcycle adventures with her husband, running, arts and crafts with her children, and gardening.

Cami is mom to four sweet kids and wife to a wonderful and supportive husband. Together, they reside in a small town in Utah. She obtained her teaching degree from BYU Idaho in family and consumer science education and is currently a work-from-home mom. She feels fortunate to stay at home with her kids while fulfilling her need for teaching, sharing, inspiring, and connecting with others through her blog *TIDBITS*, which she established in 2010. The site is full of inspiration for do-it-yourself living, home decor, recipes, and lifestyle tips. Her favorite interests include date night with her husband, flipping through magazines, running, hiking, the color white, fresh peach pie, photography, and playing with her kids.

ACKNOWLEDGMENTS

To our good husbands, who not only had the very important task of taste-testing and being our food critics, but whose support and encouragement was the reason behind it all.

Also to our husbands and children for their patience and understanding as we sacrificed a good part of our time and energy toward the making of this book.

To our amazing mother, whose example of strength and resilience gives us the courage to push ourselves, to grow, to work together, and to be the best that we can be. More importantly, her encouragement to be loving and understanding towards everyone and to give our all to the things that matter most in this life. And for whom we know is taking full credit for all the talents and abilities we possess . . . rightfully so, Mother.

To our father, who is no longer with us, but who we felt cheering us on the whole way through.

To our editor, Chamois Holschuh, whose proofreading and editing skills greatly contributed to the quality and readability of the book.

To Sandy DeGasser, our portrait photographer and dear friend, for her efforts to ease our awkwardness behind the camera and all the moral support.

To Barbara Schieving, of the blog *Pressure Cooking Today,* who has been so kind and supportive and has inspired us with her honest, ethical work. Also, for being so willing to answer our questions and see us through some challenging hurdles.

We would like to express gratitude to our friends and family who saw us through this book. Thank you for your time, love, and support. Your patience and kindness made our dream of creating this book a reality.

INTRODUCTION

My pressure cooker journey is a fun and interesting one. I knew at a very young age that the pot rattling away on the stove was called a pressure cooker, but because the only thing I ever saw it used for was potatoes, that's all I thought it was good for. I received not one, but TWO stove top pressure cookers when I got married and didn't go near them for years. One night I wanted to make mashed potatoes, so of course I pulled out the pressure cooker pot and proceeded to call my mom to learn how to use it. All I remember from what my mom taught me that day was, "Be so careful! It can explode! Don't even try to remove the lid until it's cooled down! Stay back so you don't get burned!" Needless to say, this apparently dangerous appliance got stuffed back into my cupboard to collect more dust. It came out here and there, mostly because my then-toddler daughter liked to play drums on it, but that was about it. Then one spring cleaning day, both pressure cookers went bye-bye, and I never considered using one again.

Then came a new appliance called "The Electric Pressure Cooker," and being a girl who LOVES new fancy appliances, I read about it, considered the purchase, and ultimately decided it might be a good Christmas present for my grandma and bought myself a food processor instead. It was only after my mother-in-law got one and loved it that I finally decided I needed to check it out.

I waited until I found one for a great deal and then made the purchase. Yet still, I opened it, tried to read and comprehend the manual in 2 minutes, then packed it away in the storage room. What finally pulled me back in was the day I came upon a blog called *Pressure Cooking Today*, created by an amazing lady named Barbara. Her love for the pressure cooker was infectious, and her recipes were amazing—I was hooked! With proven recipes now at my disposal, I used it several times a week. Having cooked my way through her blog, I felt as if I'd mastered the pressure cooker! Not only does the pressure cooker save me time, but it makes the flavors and texture of my foods better than ever! I went through my stash of go-to recipes and made a stack of the ones I felt could be successfully adapted to the pressure cooker. That is what brought my sister Cami and me to this point in our lives.

Cami was already running a popular home decor and DIY blog when I brought her over a quart of the most amazing yogurt I had ever made in my pressure cooker. She then got her own pressure cooker, posted the recipe on her blog, and we watched in amazement as the post really took off! We came to realize that we weren't the only ones in love with this appliance, nor were we the only ones that stared at it in confusion when we first received it.

Motivated by our own excitement of the electric pressure cooker and that of *TIDBITS* readers, we decided it would be a fun adventure to package up all our favorites in a cookbook. To add to the excitement, the possibility of getting our work published became a dream come true. To see our individual talents work together and unfold into these gorgeous pages has been rewarding for us beyond words.

My goal with this book is to give you a head start in the world of pressure cooking because I had several fails as I depended on time charts and user manuals to create good recipes. I became very frustrated with the appliance. I want to make sure beginners and even seasoned cooks start with the essential knowledge needed, as well as recipes that will delight and excite, with the desire to use and experiment with your pressure cooker even more. I've included my family's favorite recipes from over the years; some are originals, and some are recipes I've made better and easier by adapting them from my most favorite books and blogs. There are several accessories that really make using the pressure cooker even more multifunctional, and I'll be including our favorites in the book. I've also added several useful tips and tricks that I've learned throughout the years to fast-forward your journey to becoming a master chef! With each recipe there's a quick introduction, which I've had a blast writing and want to share in order to show how the food has been experienced in my own home. I find recipes most intriguing when I know the heart of them, so I hope you enjoy my own little adventures in cooking as you create your own stories.

Here is a little about my personal food and healthy eating philosophy. This has also changed dramatically over the years; after having gone from one extreme to the other in this area, this is where I am today. Food is meant to be enjoyed. Food elicits beautiful memories that are not easily forgotten. It has the ability to pull emotional strings with a smell, a taste, or a simple glance. My goal in feeding myself, my family, and my friends is to use food to create good memories and positive experiences that will last for years and years. I want to help others develop a love and enjoyment for cooking that can be shared with their loved ones as well. I choose not to dwell on what is and isn't healthy, but I do strive to use a great variety of quality foods to make cooking and eating a delightful experience for all.

That said, pull out that pressure cooker, dive into this book, and get ready to fall in love with the new and improved version of an appliance that has held its place in the homes of so many for decades! It's my hope that, as you work your way through these delicious recipes, your confidence in using the appliance will grow, and you can also master the potential of the electric pressure cooker. You will love it! I guarantee it!

—Marci

BASICS OF PRESSURE COOKING

QUICK START GUIDE

For those of you who, like me, have a total of five seconds before an impending interruption, here is your Quick Start Guide to get you going. Pull your pressure cooker out of the box, cupboard, or basement—and let's get started!

Begin with a reliable recipe (hint: this book is loaded). A pressure cooker typically needs about 1 cup of liquid in order to build pressure. This will be part of the recipe.

Once the food is inside the pot, secure the lid in place (it should be in a position where you can lift the lid handle and the lid will not come off).

Every pressure cooker has a pressure release knob on top of the lid. It needs to be in a sealed position in order to build pressure (which will be indicated by words on the knob, like "pressure" or "sealing").

Select the pressure button and adjust cook time to the number of minutes indicated in the recipe. Each model may be slightly different, but this is the basic idea.

The pressure cooker will take 10-30 minutes to come up to pressure (depending on what you're cooking), at which point it will seal shut and the cooking time will start. As a safety feature, the lid cannot be removed at this point.

When the pressure cooker beeps that the cooking is done, the pressure must be released in order to remove the lid. Next to the knob will be words like "steam" or "venting." This is the position that will release the pressure. The recipe will indicate either a "quick" or "natural" release, or a natural release followed by a quick release. "Quick" means to turn the pressure release knob to the release position and allow the pressure to rapidly release; this can take up to a minute. "Natural" means to do nothing; the pressure will slowly release as the food inside cools down, at which point the lid may be removed. Some recipes will indicate a natural release for a certain amount of time, and then after that, you will turn the knob to release the rest of the pressure rapidly.

Remove the lid, and behold your masterpiece!
Read on for more details.

WHY USE AN ELECTRIC PRESSURE COOKER?

Safety

Today's pressure cookers are nothing like the ones our parents and grandparents used. The safety features are such that there will be no surprise explosions resulting in indescribable messes or injuries.

Fast Cooking

In our increasingly fast-paced world, pressure cookers are a lifesaver. They have the potential to cut cooking times by half or more. This means higher quality meals, made more easily with less planning.

More Flavor

Pressure cooking creates an environment that preserves and concentrates the flavor of foods. Pressure infuses flavor into the food, instead of allowing it to evaporate into the air, which means marinades and seasonings don't lose their potency.

Hands-Off Cooking

Push the buttons and walk away while the pressure cooker does its thing. No need to check, stir, or adjust temperatures.

Versatility

The pressure cooker works magic on every category of food. In one appliance, you can make everything from shredded beef to chocolate cake with results that are often superior to the more traditional cooking method.

PRESSURE COOKER LINGO

High Pressure vs. Low Pressure

Most pressure cookers have a "high" and "low" option, some even have a "medium" option. While most foods are cooked at high pressure, there are some that require more gentle cooking; recipes will indicate one or the other.

Quick vs. Natural Release

When the cooking is complete, the built-up pressure needs to be released in order for the lid to be removed. This is done with either a "quick" or a "natural" release, or sometimes a combination of both. A quick release is done by carefully turning the pressure release knob to a release position. This is good for foods that are at risk of being overcooked. To do a

natural release, simply do nothing to the cooker until the pressure releases on its own and the lid is able to be removed. This works well on foods that create a lot of foam, like oats, rice, and fruit, or recipes that contain a lot of liquid, like soups and sauces. A natural release is also preferred for meat that needs a rest time for ultimate tenderness. If a recipe calls for both, let the cooker sit for the instructed amount of natural release time, and then switch the valve to release the remaining pressure. The steam coming from the cooker is extremely hot, so always release with caution.

Pressure Release Knob

This is the knob on the top of the lid that needs to be in a sealed position to build pressure and in a released position to allow pressure to escape.

Pressure Indicator

This is a float valve located near the pressure release knob that will pop up when the pot has reached the correct pressure and will drop down when the pressure is released. It will make a small click sound when it drops.

EXTRA PRESSURE COOKING TIPS

- Don't overfill the cooker! There is a "max fill line" inside the pot—follow the guideline. Generally speaking, fruit, beans, rice, and grains should fill no more than half of the pot, and for everything else (meat, soups, vegetables, etc.), fill no more than two-thirds full.

- Use the oven broiler to finish things off. This is a quick way to melt cheese or brown and crisp your final product.

- Add citrus and herbs after cooking is complete. This will give brightness and freshness to your food.

- When releasing pressure using the quick method, if liquid starts spraying through the valve, flip it back to a sealed position and allow your food to cool for 5–10 minutes before trying again.

- If more cooking is required after the lid is removed (for example, undercooked chicken, crunchy potatoes, etc.), ensure there is still at least 1 cup of liquid in the pot, secure the lid, and add extra cooking time. With the contents of the pot already hot, the pressure will build, and the cooker will seal very quickly.

- Use cooking charts as a guideline, but allow for adjustments. Depending on the size, temperature, and quality of your food, timing may vary. This is especially true with meat. A quick internet search will reveal twenty different ways to cook a chicken breast or a chuck roast. I've done a LOT of testing to know which times work well for me and know which local stores provide consistently good quality meat. Be flexible as you learn what works best for you. If a specific cooking method doesn't produce the desired results, keep experimenting!

- With most recipes, doubling and tripling the recipe rarely means that the cooking time needs to be increased.

- To build pressure, a cooker needs a certain amount of liquid. In most cases, this is about 1 cup; however, some foods release liquid as they are heated, so they may not require as much initial liquid. Foods that cook for 30 minutes or more, that don't create their own juices, may require more than 1 cup of liquid before cooking is started.

- Most pressure cookers have several functions that make it truly an all-in-one appliance. Functions may include yogurt, steam, slow cook, sauté, brown, etc. This means extra steps like sautéing onions, browning meat, or boiling pasta can all be done in the same pot. Read its manual to discover its full potential.

- Because there isn't evaporation in a sealed pressure cooker, sauces may not thicken inside the cooker. Use the sauté or brown function to reduce sauces, or use a thickener like cornstarch after the pressure cooking is complete.
- Read the manual for cleaning instructions, so your pressure cooker continues to cook and build pressure as intended.
- Have two silicone seals: one for potent, savory smells and one for delicate, neutral, or sweet smells to prevent crossover in taste.
- Removing the food smells from the silicone seal can be a challenge, but here are a few methods to try:
  - scrub with soap and water, and store upside down to air out
  - remove seal from the lid, and wash in the dishwasher on the top shelf
  - place seal in direct sunlight for several hours
  - place a bowl of baking soda inside the pot and place the lid on top
  - soak in 1 part vinegar and 2 parts water
  - place lemons and water inside pot, and cook at high pressure for 2 minutes.
- Finally, keep in mind that one of the wonderful things about pressure cookers is that they make faster work of many recipes; however, this isn't always the case. In some instances, if you add up how long it takes to build and release pressure, the time ends up being about the same. One of the greatest advantages of electric pressure cookers is that they make cooking much simpler and hands-off. With the press of a button, food will cook without checking, stirring, or adjusting of temperatures. Results are often superior in the pressure cooker as well. Pressure cookers don't heat up the kitchen like an oven or stove top, and they are also portable (the perfect appliance for campers!). Another perk is that, if distractions occur and your food is forgotten, it's not going to overflow on the stove top or burn in the oven. It will simply be kept warm inside the pressure cooker pot.
- For more pressure cooking recipes or tips, visit some of my favorite sites:
  - tidbits-marci.com
  - tidbits-cami.com
  - pressurecookingtoday.com
  - hippressurecooking.com
  - melskitchencafe.com

RECOMMENDED PRODUCTS

ACCESSORIES

Mesh Steamer Basket

Fine Mesh Strainer

Collapsible Steamer Basket

6-inch Square Pans

7-inch Springform Pan/Mini
Springform Pans

8-inch Pushpan

8-inch Perforated Pan

6-cup Bundt Pan

3–4-inch Heating Core

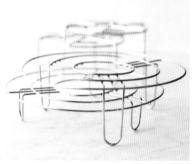

Trivets (variety of different heights)

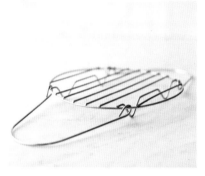

Trivet with Handles

6-ounce Ramekins

1½-quart Heat-Safe Baking Dish/16-ounce Round Heat-Safe Baking Dish

Heat-Safe Glass Bowl

Euro Cuisine® Yogurt Strainer

Mason Jar Jacket

Mason Jar Lid/Pour Cap

FOOD PRODUCTS

Westbrae Natural® Organic
  Unsweetened Ketchup
http://www.westbrae.com

Sir Kensington's Chipotle Mayo
http://sirkensingtons.com

HERDEZ® Tomatillo Verde Sauce
http://www.herdeztraditions.com

Franks® Red Hot Buffalo Wings Sauce
https://www.franksredhot.com

Lindt Excellence Chocolate Bars
http://www.lindtusa.com

Ghirardelli® Chocolate Melting Wafers
https://www.ghirardelli.com

Madagascar Bourbon Vanilla Beans
https://www.beanilla.com

King Arthur® Vietnamese Cinnamon
http://www.kingarthurflour.com

Dang® Coconut Chips
http://dangfoods.com

Fage® Total 2% Yogurt
http://usa.fage

Boursin® Herb Cheese
http://www.boursin.com/en_us

Cacique® Queso Quesadilla Cheese
http://www.caciqueinc.com

Supremo® Queso Chihuahua Quesadilla Cheese
http://www.vvsupremo.com

Tinkyada® Brown Rice Pasta
http://www.tinkyada.com

Smirnoff® Vodka 80 Proof
http://www.smirnoff.com

CrioBru™
https://www.criobru.com

RECIPE ADAPTATIONS

We love to give credit where credit is due! While we thrive on creating our own original recipes, the following list represents some of our favorite bloggers and online sites that have created a recipe we loved, which we have taken and adapted it for the pressure cooker, putting our own spin on it. We highly encourage you to take a look at these sites and the correlating recipes from our book, then study and compare the two. By doing this, you will learn how easy it is to take a recipe you love and turn it into a pressure-cooker dish. This will be a huge help for you in learning how to master the pressure cooker yourself!

Annies-eats.com
Spring Green Risotto
http://www.annies-eats.com/2010/03/30/spring-green-risotto/

Bakingbites.com
White Chocolate Vanilla Lava Cake
http://bakingbites.com/2015/01/white-chocolate-lava-cakes/

Carlsbadcravings.com
Sweet Curry Coconut Cashew Rice
http://www.carlsbadcravings.com/pineapple-coconut-cashew-rice/

Feelgreatin8.com
Coconut Vanilla Syrup
http://blog.feelgreatin8.com/homemade-caramel-sauce/

Gimmesomeoven.com
Quinoa Pizza Bowls
http://www.gimmesomeoven.com/easy-quinoa-pizza-bowls/

Helynskitchen.com
Vanilla Cashew Cream "Cheesecake" with Cherry Compote
http://helynskitchen.com/2013/10/date-sweetened-vegan-pumpkin-pie.html

Hippressurecooking.com

Spiced Poached Pears
http://www.hippressurecooking.com/red-wine-stewed-pears-fruity-sweet/

Zucchini Pesto Sauce
http://www.hippressurecooking.com/zucchin-pesto-pressure-cooker-recipe/

Iowagirleats.com

Cauliflower Gnocchi Soup with White Cheddar Crisps
http://iowagirleats.com/2015/12/02/roasted-cauliflower-and-potato-soup/

Chicken with Cheesy Herb Sauce on Rice
http://iowagirleats.com/2013/05/20/creamy-chicken-and-herb-skillet/

Pepperoncini Beef Sandwich with Chopped Giardiniera
http://iowagirleats.com/2013/10/23/crock-pot-italian-beef-sandwiches/

Joyfulhealthyeats.com

Mongolian Beef with Quick Pickled Vegetables
http://www.joyfulhealthyeats.com/honey-sriracha-mongolian-beef-with-rice-noodles/

Kingarthurflour.com

Lemon Blueberry Breakfast Cake
http://www.kingarthurflour.com/recipes/blueberry-breakfast-cake-recipe

Melskitchencafe.com

Chocolate Fudge Lava Cake
http://www.melskitchencafe.com/my-favorite-chocolate-molten-lava-cakes/

Cheesy Butternut Squash Ravioli Soup
http://www.melskitchencafe.com/slow-cooker-butternut-squash-tortellini/

Creamy Enchilada Soup
http://www.melskitchencafe.com/the-best-chicken-enchilada-soup/

Creamy Zucchini Spinach Soup
http://www.melskitchencafe.com/creamy-spinach-soup/

Pork Burrito Bowls
http://www.melskitchencafe.com/slow-cooker-pork-carnitas/

Orwhateveryoudo.com

Barbecue Sauce
http://www.orwhateveryoudo.com/2014/07/homemade-barbecue-sauce.html

Pinchofyum.com
Cauliflower Fettuccine Alfredo

http://pinchofyum.com/creamy-cauliflower-sauce

Mean Green Mac and Cheese

http://pinchofyum.com/5-minute-magic-green-sauce

Spinach and Garbanzo Bean Stuffed Sweet Potato

http://pinchofyum.com/healthy-sweet-potato-skins

Teriyaki Sauce

http://pinchofyum.com/30-minute-sesame-mango-chicken-teriyaki

Pressurecookingtoday.com
Berries and Cream Breakfast Cake

http://www.pressurecookingtoday.com/pressure-cooker-berry-compote/

Cinnamon Vanilla Applesauce

http://www.pressurecookingtoday.com/pressure-cooker-applesauce/

Mini Frittatas

http://www.pressurecookingtoday.com/egg-muffins-in-the-pressure-cooker/

Skinnytaste.com
Buttermilk and Chive Mashed Potatoes

http://www.skinnytaste.com/skinny-buttermilk-mashed-potatoes-with/

Marinara Sauce

http://www.skinnytaste.com/quick-marinara-sauce/

Thesisterscafe.com
Curry Coconut Lime Chicken Tenders

http://www.thesisterscafe.com/2012/06/7331

Rainbow Thai Soup

http://www.thesisterscafe.com/2013/03/thai-coconut-lime-soup

Wellplated.com
Caribbean Chicken Lettuce Wraps with Mango Citrus Dressing

http://www.wellplated.com/caribbean-chicken-salad/

Honey Glazed Carrots

http://www.wellplated.com/crock-pot-honey-carrots/

Womansday.com
Triple Layer Chocolate Cheesecake

http://www.womansday.com/food-recipes/food-drinks/recipes/a10516/triple-chocolate-cheesecake-122011/

BREAKFAST

Apple Cinnamon Walnut Custard Steel Cut Oats

As a child, I felt so proud to be able to pull out a packet of instant oatmeal and "cook" breakfast for myself. My mom would buy the variety pack, and I knew I had to get to it before anyone else if I wanted to hoard the most prized flavor of the box: Apple Cinnamon. I'd sneak all but one pack (didn't want to look suspicious or anything) and stuff it far back into the pantry along with the mini boxes of marshmallow cereal I was also hiding from my siblings. (I had five siblings, including three brothers who refused to heed the "I touched it first" rule.) This Apple Cinnamon Walnut Custard Oatmeal is the grown-up, healthy version of that prized little packet, and it is incredible! It is creamy, perfectly sweet with juicy bites of apples and raisins, and the joyful crunch of walnuts. Although, I feel it's only fair to keep my promise to my daughter and tell you she did NOT approve of the walnuts. To each their own!

• •

Prep: 15 minutes
Pressure: 40 minutes
Total: 70 minutes

Pressure Level: High
Release: 10-minute natural
Serves: 5-6

• •

Ingredients

1⅔ cups milk
1 cup applesauce (see page 201)
1 cup steel-cut oats
1 cup peeled, chopped apple
⅓ cup maple syrup
½ cup golden raisins
⅓ cup chopped walnuts
2 eggs, beaten
2 teaspoons cinnamon
1 teaspoon baking powder
1 teaspoon vanilla extract
¼ teaspoon salt

> This oatmeal can be made up to 3 days in advance and stored in the fridge. Stir well before placing it inside the pressure cooker pot to cook. This oatmeal doesn't cook up quick, but when prepped beforehand, it makes for a super easy, healthy breakfast.

Directions

1. Lightly spray a 1½-quart or larger heat-safe baking dish with nonstick cooking spray and set aside. To a large mixing bowl, add all of the ingredients and mix well. Pour mixture into the prepared baking dish.

2. Add 1½ cups of water to the pressure cooker pot and place trivet inside. Place dish on the trivet using a silicone or tinfoil sling to make for easier removal. Secure the lid and turn pressure cooker knob to a sealed position. Cook at high pressure for 40 minutes.

3. When cooking is complete, use a natural release for 10 minutes and then release any remaining pressure.

4. Stir the oatmeal and serve hot with a Frozen Whipped Cream Dollop (page 189), cream, or milk.

> Omit walnuts or sprinkle them on top of individual bowls just before serving if needed to make all diners happy.

Berries and Cream Breakfast Cake

There once was a time when I could tell my kids we were having breakfast cake in the morning and their eyes would sparkle, they'd smile from ear to ear, and at least one of them would ask, "Is it somebody's birthday?" Well, the magic is gone now. I've tested at least twenty-seven different versions of this cake; the sparkly eyes have turned into groans and overly dramatic collapses to the floor. Not to be defeated, I searched my brain for the prettiest, yummiest breakfast cake version I could think of, drizzled it with "frosting," and as the kids started to come downstairs for breakfast, I yelled, "Who wants Christmas Cake!" . . . and just like that, I'm back to best-mommy-ever status. Made in a decorative Bundt pan, swirled with a divine berry compote, and drizzled with a sweet yogurt glaze, this cake is loaded with protein and whole grains— and is officially back among the Top 5 Breakfast Requests

Prep: 10 minutes
Pressure: 25 minutes
Total: 45 minutes

Pressure Level: High
Release: 10-minute natural
Serves: 4-6

For Berry Compote
2 cups blueberries
1 cup sliced strawberries
zest of 1 lemon
⅓ cup pure maple syrup, or honey
1 tablespoon cornstarch
1 tablespoon water

> The compote is best made the day before and used cold. This recipe makes more than needed for this cake.

Directions for the Berry Compote

1. Prepare the Berry Compote beforehand so it is cold and thick. (If used warm, it has a tendency to sink to the bottom of the pan.) Add blueberries, strawberries, lemon zest, and maple syrup to the pressure cooker pot and stir. Secure the lid and turn pressure release knob to a sealed position. Cook at high pressure for 3 minutes.

2. When cooking is complete, use a natural release for 10 minutes and then release any remaining pressure.

3. In a small bowl, whisk together cornstarch and water. Select sauté on the pressure cooker and bring berry mixture to a light boil. While whisking, pour cornstarch mixture into the berry mixture and whisk constantly until compote thickens. Cool and store in a sealed container in the fridge.

For Breakfast Cake
5 eggs
¼ cup sugar
2 tablespoons butter, melted
¾ cup ricotta cheese
¾ cup plain or vanilla yogurt
2 teaspoons vanilla extract
1 cup whole wheat pastry flour, or white whole wheat flour
½ teaspoon salt
2 teaspoons baking powder
½ cup Berry Compote
Sweet Yogurt Glaze

Directions for the Breakfast Cake

1. Generously grease a 6-cup Bundt pan with nonstick cooking spray; set aside.

2. Beat together eggs and sugar until smooth. Add the butter, ricotta cheese, yogurt, and vanilla; continue mixing until smooth.

3. In a separate bowl, whisk together the flour, salt, and baking powder. Combine with the egg mixture. Pour into the prepared Bundt pan.

4. Using ½ cup of Berry Compote, drop by tablespoons on top of the batter and swirl in with a knife.

5. Add 1 cup of water to the pressure cooker pot and place a trivet inside. Carefully place the Bundt pan on the trivet.

6. Secure the lid and turn pressure release knob to a sealed position. Cook at high pressure for 25 minutes.

7. When pressure cooking is complete, use a natural release for 10 minutes and then release any remaining pressure.

8. Remove pan from pressure cooker. Cool slightly. Loosen the sides of the cake from the pan and gently turn over onto a plate.

9. Drizzle with Sweet Yogurt Glaze and serve warm.

For Sweet Yogurt Glaze

¼ cup yogurt
½ teaspoon vanilla extract
1 teaspoon milk
1-2 tablespoons powdered sugar

Directions for the Sweet Yogurt Glaze

1. To make the Sweet Yogurt Glaze, whisk together the yogurt, vanilla, milk, and powdered sugar; set aside until ready to drizzle over cake.

To make removal of the pan easier, create a tinfoil sling by folding a piece of tinfoil into thirds. The foil must be long enough to fit around the base of the Bundt pan. The Bundt pan will sit on top of the tinfoil with a piece of foil coming up on both sides. Fold the side pieces down as needed, so as not to interfere with the lid. When cake is done, grab the sides of the foil and lift pan from the pot.

Breakfast Peach Cobbler

After the birth of my twin boys, I took an online course called "Go Sugar Free." Something about the stress of taking care of a potty-training two year old and two newborns (one of which was extremely colicky) drove me daily to my secret chocolate stash and nightly to a big bowl of ice cream. However, I look back on those years and want to give my past self a high-five and tell her, "You go girl! Go ahead and have that giant bowl of mint chocolate chip ice cream! Now top it with Oreos and a fat drizzle of caramel and go to your happy place!" I honestly can't say that I regret my indulgences one bit, but when I was ready to be done with my slightly less than ideal coping methods, it took this life-changing course (created by Jacqueline Smith, one of the most wonderful individuals I've ever known) to kick my sugar habit to the curb.

I now maintain a naturally or very minimally sweetened lifestyle and, because of it, have become a better cook. Another bonus is that I no longer have to hide my chocolate stash because my family won't go near my 90–95% cacao bars! So, my point . . . while desserts no longer appeal to me, peach cobbler somehow has never lost its delicious appeal, so I set out to make a version that I could enjoy every day for breakfast. This dish marries a perfectly moist zucchini cornbread topping (yay for getting a vegetable into my children before they've even changed out of PJs!) with a juicy, sweet explosion of the greatest fruit of all time: PEACHES . . . obviously, right?! I like to transfer it steaming hot to a different bowl (sorry if you haven't yet burned all the heat sensitivity out of your fingertips—you're about to) with a splash of cold milk. Just like that, I'm taken back to hot summer days as a carefree kid . . . sigh . . . found my happy place again.

Prep: 10 minutes
Pressure: 15 minutes
Total: 30 minutes

Pressure Level: High
Release: Quick
Serves: Up to 12

Ingredients

medium-sized peaches, peeled and chopped
  (1 for each ramekin) (may substitute thawed frozen peaches)
2 cups unpeeled zucchini, shredded
1 cup yellow cornmeal
1 cup whole wheat pastry flour, or white whole wheat flour
¼–⅓ cup sugar
1 tablespoon baking powder
¼ teaspoon baking soda
¾ teaspoon salt
1 cup buttermilk
2 eggs, lightly beaten
4 tablespoons butter, melted

> The cobbler can be eaten out of the ramekin as is, or carefully transferred to a larger single-serving bowl and filled with a little milk. Enjoy with a light drizzle of honey or a sprinkle of cinnamon sugar.

Directions

1. Lightly grease desired number of ramekins with nonstick cooking spray. Set aside.

2. Place zucchini in a colander. Press and squeeze to drain as much liquid as possible. This can also be done by putting zucchini inside a nut milk bag. Twist and squeeze to remove excess moisture.

3. Fill each ramekin with 1 chopped peach. Optional: Drizzle peach slices lightly with honey if they aren't very ripe or sweet.

4. In a medium bowl, stir together the cornmeal, flour, sugar, baking powder, baking soda, and salt.

5. In a separate small bowl, whisk together buttermilk and eggs. Whisk quickly while pouring in the melted butter, to incorporate well. Then stir in drained zucchini.

6. Pour buttermilk mixture into the dry ingredients and stir just until combined.

7. Using a ¼-cup cookie scoop (or measuring cup), top each of the peach filled ramekins with about ¼ cup of batter, spreading it slightly so it touches the sides of the ramekin.

8. Add 1 cup of water to the pressure cooker pot and place trivet inside. Place three ramekins on the trivet. A second trivet can be placed on top to accommodate another layer of three ramekins (a total of six can be cooked at a time). Secure the lid and turn pressure release knob to a sealed position. Cook at high pressure for 15 minutes.

9. When cooking is complete, use a quick release. Serve immediately.

This recipe makes enough batter for 12 ramekins, but only 6 ramekins will fit in the pressure cooker at one time. Either prepare the ramekins in two batches, or make desired number of ramekins and store the remaining batter in the refrigerator for up to 4 days. This makes for a quick and easy breakfast.

Cinnamon Swirl Peach Breakfast Cake

As I neared the end of recipe-creating for this cookbook, I flipped through the pages and had a small moment of panic as I thought, Have I gone too far with peach recipes? Is that even possible? But what about my dream of cinnamon brown sugar French toast topped with peaches? That must be turned into a breakfast cake, right? I ignored the pessimistic peach doubter in my mind and brought my breakfast dream to life (breakfast dreams are a sign of higher intelligence, right?!). I mixed up my basic breakfast batter, stirred in my last three peaches, and swirled in a heavenly combination of dark brown sugar and King Arthur Vietnamese Cinnamon (you've never had cinnamon this potent and sweet, I promise)—and my favorite breakfast cake was born. Still, I wondered, can a cookbook use too many peaches? As I watched my kids cry, steal, and negotiate chores for the final piece of cake, I thought . . . nope. Besides, salt is used in my recipes way more times than peaches. This recipe is a keeper!

Prep: 10 minutes
Pressure: 40 minutes
Total: 60 minutes

Pressure Level: High
Release: 10-minute natural
Serves: 4-6

Ingredients

5 eggs
2 tablespoons butter, melted
¾ cup ricotta cheese
¾ cup plain or vanilla yogurt
2 teaspoons vanilla extract
1 cup whole wheat pastry flour, or white whole wheat flour
½ teaspoon salt
2 teaspoons baking powder
1½ cups chopped peaches (fresh, canned, or thawed frozen)
¼ cup brown sugar
2 teaspoons cinnamon (preferably King Arthur® Vietnamese cinnamon)
additional cinnamon sugar, for serving (optional)

Directions

1. Grease a 7-inch springform pan with nonstick cooking spray.

2. Whisk eggs in a medium bowl. Add the butter, ricotta cheese, yogurt, and vanilla. Mix until smooth.

3. In a separate bowl, stir together the flour, salt, and baking powder; combine with egg mixture. Pour into the prepared springform pan. Scatter peaches over the top.

4. Combine brown sugar and cinnamon; sprinkle on top of the batter. Use a knife to swirl the cinnamon sugar into the cake.

5. Add 1 cup of water to the pressure cooker pot and place a trivet inside. Carefully place the springform pan on the trivet.

6. Secure the lid and turn pressure release knob to a sealed position. Cook at high pressure for 40 minutes.

7. When cooking is complete, use a natural release for 10 minutes and then release any remaining pressure.

8. Remove pan from pressure cooker. Carefully remove the springform ring. If it is sticking, run a knife around the edges of the cake to loosen.

9. Sprinkle with additional cinnamon sugar, if desired, and brown under the oven broiler. Serve warm.

Coconut Vanilla Syrup

I love making breakfast. There are so many fun recipes for breakfast and so many opportunities to incorporate whole grains, seeds, nuts, fruit, protein, etc. But then out comes the river of syrup that pours over my loved ones' omega-6 fatty acid–rich pancakes, and I wonder to myself why I stress so much about the tiny suckers my kids get offered every time we run an errand. Is it possible for syrup to be healthy? Or at least healthier? Why, yes, it is. This syrup made with a combination of pure maple syrup and coconut milk is perfectly sweet, smooth, and dreamy over pancakes, waffles, and yogurt, or even as a fruit dip. With the many health benefits of coconut milk, I no longer mind a little syrup indulgence. Now go make some flax seed waffles!

Prep: 1 minute
Pressure: 10 minutes
Total: 20 minutes

Pressure Level: High
Release: Quick
Makes: About 2 cups

Ingredients

14-ounce can lite unsweetened coconut milk
½ cup pure maple syrup
pinch of kosher salt
1 tablespoon vanilla extract

> For an amazing variation, add 2-4 cinnamon sticks at the beginning with the milk and syrup!

Directions

1. Add coconut milk, maple syrup, salt, and vanilla to the pressure cooker pot. Whisk until combined. Secure the lid and turn pressure release knob to a sealed position. Cook at high pressure for 10 minutes.

2. When cooking is complete, use a quick release.

3. Using the sauté function, simmer 5–10 minutes, stirring often, to thicken slightly. Pour into a mason jar and top with a mason jar pour cap. Use immediately or store in refrigerator for a later time. Shake well before each use.

> For an even more intense vanilla flavor, split a vanilla bean and add it to the syrup and milk in the first step. When cooking is complete, whisk the syrup and remove the vanilla bean pod. The smell is heavenly!

The pans will hold up to 2 avocados each, so it's easy to double this recipe if needed.

Use leftover avocado to make guacamole, or freeze and add to smoothies for a boost of healthy fat and creaminess.

Ham-Wrapped Avocado Egg and Creamy Lemon Sauce with Burst Parmesan Tomatoes

Watching cooking shows is my favorite way of distracting myself from the monotony of treadmill running in the mornings. One particular morning, I was watching Rachael Ray and her creation of a poached egg inside of a whole avocado, wrapped in bacon, and dredged in a buttery hollandaise sauce. "Wow," I thought, "that looks delicious," and then "Wow, I would need a morning nap after eating that." So my mind went to work on a warm, runny egg cradled in half of an avocado, wrapped in salty ham, and drizzled with a creamy lemon sauce. Suddenly, I looked down at the console of my treadmill and was stunned to see that I had already finished my six-mile run. So I happily jumped off, jotted down my new recipe idea, and headed off to the kitchen to make a masterpiece! The combination of golden egg yolk, plus tangy lemon sauce, plus warm and cheesy tomato juice is the absolute perfect combination and will set your morning off just right—no nap required.

Prep: 10 minutes
Pressure: 3–4 minutes
Total: 20 minutes

Pressure Level: Low
Release: Quick
Serves: 2

For Avocado Egg
2 large ripe avocados
4 slices thinly cut deli ham
2 eggs
salt and pepper

For Parmesan Tomatoes
1 cup grape or cherry tomatoes
2 tablespoons Parmesan cheese
¼ teaspoon Italian seasoning
¼ teaspoon garlic powder
salt and pepper

For Lemon Sauce
½ cup mayonnaise with olive oil
   (can substitute with regular mayonnaise)
½ teaspoon Dijon mustard
juice of 1 lemon
2 tablespoons melted butter
pinch of kosher salt
¼ teaspoon cayenne pepper

Directions

1. Cut off a third of the avocado lengthwise. Set aside the small end for another use. Remove the stone from the larger piece and hollow out the hole to allow an egg to fit inside. Using a large spoon, gently scoop the avocado flesh out of the skin in one piece. Slice off a small piece from the rounded side of the avocado, so it will sit without wobbling. Be very careful not to puncture the avocado (you don't want the egg to leak out!).

2. Inside a 6-inch square pan (or ramekin), overlap 2 pieces of ham lengthwise (long enough to wrap around the avocado). Place avocado on top of the ham. Crack an egg into the hollowed-out avocado. Season with salt and pepper and then wrap the ham over the top. Add half of the tomatoes to the pan or ramekin and sprinkle them with half of the cheese and seasonings. Repeat the process in another pan or ramekin for the second avocado.

3. Add 1 cup of water to the pressure cooker pot and place trivet inside. Place the prepared pans inside, stacking them to form an X shape; if using ramekins, place them side by side or stack them on top of one another by placing another trivet between them. Secure the lid and turn pressure release knob to a sealed position. Cook at low pressure for 3–4 minutes.

4. While eggs are cooking, prepare the lemon sauce by whisking mayonnaise, Dijon, and lemon juice until smooth. Quickly whisk in melted butter. Add a splash of milk or extra lemon juice to loosen it up, if needed. Season with a good pinch of kosher salt and cayenne pepper. Whisk again to combine.

5. When pressure cooking is complete, use a quick release. Egg yolk should be soft and the whites set. If not done, return to the pot, secure the lid, and cook for 1–2 more minutes at low pressure.

6. To serve, press on tomatoes lightly with a fork to get juices flowing around the avocado. Drizzle the lemon sauce over the avocado egg and season with extra salt and pepper if desired.

Ham, Spinach, and Cheddar Ramekin Eggs

I have a confession to make. I've never had this dish for breakfast, which makes me feel a little guilty about putting it in the breakfast section, but hear me out. I don't love the breakfast-pancakes-French-toast-and-waffles-for-dinner idea. My brain thinks it needs something more savory for dinner. While my meat-loving husband has got my back on this one, my kids wholeheartedly disagree. So the compromise for breakfast-as-dinner is now a healthy version of an apple crisp and these super simple, super satisfying ramekin eggs.

Prep: 10 minutes
Pressure: 3–5 minutes
Total: 20 minutes

Pressure Level: Low
Release: Quick
Serves: 6

Ingredients

1 tablespoon butter
4 tablespoons minced yellow onion
salt
pepper
4 cups spinach, coarsely chopped

¾ cup chopped ham
6 eggs
¾ cup shredded cheddar cheese
6 tablespoons heavy cream

Directions

1. Spray six 6-ounce ramekins with cooking spray and set aside.

2. Using the sauté function of the pressure cooker, melt butter until it starts to foam. Add onion and season with salt and pepper; cook until softened (about 3 minutes). Add spinach and cook until wilted (about 2 minutes). Move to another plate and set aside.

3. Divide chopped ham evenly among ramekins. Drain liquid from spinach-and-onion mixture and divide evenly among ramekins. Crack an egg into each and season with salt and pepper. Top each with a sprinkle of cheese and 1 tablespoon of cream.

4. Add 1 cup of water to the pressure cooker pot and place trivet inside. Place three ramekins on the trivet. Top with a second trivet, followed by the other three ramekins. Secure the lid and turn pressure release knob to a sealed position. Cook at low pressure for 3–5 minutes, depending on whether you prefer a runny or soft-cooked yolk.

5. When cooking is complete, use a quick release. Check eggs; if white is not set, cook an extra 1–2 minutes. Optional: Serve eggs with buttered toast for dipping.

> Take these to the next level by placing a couple tomato slices on top. Yum!

Lemon Blueberry Breakfast Cake

Every morning as a kid, breakfast consisted of the same old boring, low-sugar, zero-fiber cereals. Every now and again if my mom really wanted to rock our worlds, there would be high-sugar, artificially colored, zero-fiber cereal. Occasionally Mom would make us a breakfast of eggs, bacon, pancakes, etc., but then my sister and I would complain that we were the stinky breakfast kids on the bus. So naturally, my mom opted to sleep in and let us take care of ourselves. I was always hungry within a couple hours of being at school and can distinctly remember high school reading class at 10:30 a.m. with my stomach growling loudly, while everyone else was silently reading. As a teenager, I couldn't imagine anything more humiliating! My goal at breakfast time now is to feed my family something that will keep them satisfied and energized until lunch time. This Lemon Blueberry Breakfast Cake does a wondrous job. Jam-packed with fiber, protein, and just the right amount of sweetness, this cake will keep your family full and focused all morning. Since my mom is going to read this, I can't say that I blame her. If my kids complained about good homemade breakfasts, you bet your buns I would be snoozing away too! Love you mom!

Prep: 10 minutes
Pressure: 40 minutes
Total: 60 minutes

Pressure Level: High
Release: 10-minute natural
Serves: About 6

Ingredients

5 eggs
¼ cup sugar
2 tablespoons melted butter
¾ cup ricotta cheese
¾ cup plain or vanilla yogurt
zest of 1 lemon
2 teaspoons vanilla extract
1 cup whole wheat pastry flour, or white whole wheat flour
½ teaspoon salt
2 teaspoon baking powder
1 cup fresh blueberries
maple syrup or turbinado sugar, for topping

> Optional: Sprinkle with turbinado sugar and place under the broiler until caramelized.

> Frozen blueberries slow down the cooking process of this cake. If using frozen, add 5–10 minutes cook time.

Directions

1. Lightly grease a 7-inch springform pan with nonstick cooking spray.

2. Beat together the eggs and sugar until smooth. Add the butter, ricotta cheese, yogurt, lemon zest, and vanilla until well combined.

3. In a separate bowl, whisk together the flour, salt, and baking powder. Combine with egg mixture. Gently fold in blueberries. Pour the batter into the prepared pan.

4. Add 1 cup of water to the pressure cooker pot and place a trivet inside. Carefully set the springform pan on the trivet.

5. Secure the lid and turn pressure release knob to a sealed position. Cook at high pressure for 40 minutes.

6. When cooking is complete, use a natural release for 10 minutes and then release any remaining pressure.

7. Remove pan from pressure cooker. Carefully remove the springform ring. If it is sticking, run a knife around the edges of the cake to loosen. Serve warm as is, or with a drizzle of maple syrup.

> To speed things up in the morning, mix all the wet ingredients in a bowl the night before, cover, and refrigerate. Place dry ingredients in a quart-size resealable bag. In the morning, dump dry ingredients into the wet ingredients, mix, and then stir in blueberries.

Mason Jar Breakfast Casserole

After my "super cool wife" status started to fade after repeated Mason Jar Steel Cut Oat breakfasts (page 23), I had to come up with something else exciting that I could pack my husband on his way out the door in the mornings. Meet Mason Jar Breakfast Casserole. Before we discuss its potentials, I feel a need to apologize to my mom for saying "Casseroles are so 1995." Sorry, Mom, you're never wrong. Now, potentials . . . so many! Kid favorites around here are cheddar-bacon-spinach and-sausage-plus-syrup. My hubby and I load ours with sausage, peppers, jalapeño, pepper jack cheese, and a gallon of hot sauce. It's also a great way to use up leftover bits of meat and veggies in your fridge. I haven't found anything that hasn't worked yet. (Okay, my son's pomegranate seeds-and-raisin version was questionable, but not terrible.) Sky's the limit here–dream big!

Prep: 10 minutes
Pressure: 10 minutes
Total: 25 minutes

Pressure Level: High
Release: 2-minute natural
Serves: 1 (1 mason jar per person)

Ingredients

½ cup cooked, grated potato
salt and pepper
⅓ cup extras, such as diced raw or cooked veggies (bell pepper, onion, mushroom, jalapeño, etc.), cooked crumbled sausage or bacon, diced ham, etc.
2 eggs, beaten with fork
1-2 tablespoons cheese (pepper jack, cheddar, mozzarella, etc.)
optional toppings: salsa, ketchup, hot sauce, maple syrup, herbs, etc.

> Awesome tip from my sister Maegan: Prep your potatoes and sausage all at once in the pressure cooker! Wrap potatoes in foil and place them inside a steamer or on top of a trivet alongside 1 pound of uncooked sausage. Cook at high pressure for 25 minutes with a 10-minute natural release.

Directions

1. Spray the inside of a half-pint mason jar with nonstick cooking spray. Add grated potato to the jar and press flat. Season with salt and pepper. Add desired extras. Pour in eggs, then season with more salt and pepper as desired. Top with a sprinkle of cheese.

2. Add 1 cup of water to the pressure cooker pot and place a trivet inside. Place uncovered jar on the trivet. Secure the lid and turn pressure release knob to a sealed position. Cook at high pressure for 10 minutes.

3. When cooking is complete, use a natural release for 2 minutes and then release any remaining pressure.

4. Add desired toppings and serve. Caution: Jar will be hot!

> ### Tips
> - Use a mason jar jacket to make this a handheld, on-the-go breakfast.
> - Make up your jars the night before for a well-balanced, easy breakfast the next morning.
> - If adding more extras, use a pint-size mason jar and cook for the same amount of time.
> - A 6-quart pressure cooker will fit up to six half-pint jars and three pint-size jars, so increase the number of servings as needed.
> - The casserole cooks more quickly and evenly with multiple jars in the pot. If only cooking a single casserole, add 1-2 more jars (containing just water) inside the pot.

Mason Jar Steel Cut Oats

Remember how, as a kid, you dreamed about being a famous rock star, actress, or athlete? Well . . . I never became famous for any of those things. But guess what: I am famous for oatmeal. You see, my husband's famous for his serious skills on a dirt bike, and because of him and his endless praise of me and my cooking, I'm now famous for my steel cut oat-making skills. The perfect combination of chewy steel cut oats, maple syrup, fruit, spices, and chia seeds has made me an all-star. My husband claims that there is no better breakfast for fueling him for a rigorous workday or an exhausting dirt bike adventure. To make this a quick and easy on-the-go breakfast for him (and oh yeah, for his buddies that now request it), I adapted it to a single-serving jar. It has been a major hit! So while I should be famous for my singing (no I shouldn't), I'm proud to be famous for SSCOS—Serious Steel Cut Oat Skills.

Prep: 5–10 minutes
Pressure: 20 minutes
Total: 30–40 minutes

Pressure: High
Release: 10-minute natural
Serves: 1 (1 mason jar per person)

Ingredients
¼ cup steel cut oats
2 tablespoons pure maple syrup
1–2 teaspoons chia seeds
pinch of salt
½ cup extras (variations on the next few pages)
about 1 cup room-temperature water
1 Frozen Whipped Cream Dollop (page 189)

> If your pressure cooker has a delay function, prepare oats the night before (omitting the fruit), set inside pot, and set the timer to start cooking an hour before you're ready to eat. With zero morning effort on your part, the oats will be cooked, rested, cooled, and ready for fruit and a big dollop of frozen cream!

Directions

1. Add oats, syrup, chia seeds, salt, and extras to a pint-size wide-mouth mason jar. Add water, leaving 1½ inches of headspace. Tightly screw on flat and metal ring. Shake until everything is well distributed and the chia seeds aren't clumping together.

2. Unscrew and again tighten just until the lid meets resistance (fingertip tight).

3. Add 1 cup of water to the pressure cooker pot and place a short trivet inside (if the rack is too tall, the pressure cooker lid will not close properly over the jars). Place jar on the trivet. Secure the lid and turn pressure release knob to a sealed position. Cook at high pressure for 20 minutes.

4. When cooking is complete, use a natural release for 10 minutes and then release any remaining pressure. Remove the jar from the pot and place on a cooling rack or hot pad. Caution: The jar will be very hot! Do not open the jar until contents have settled (no longer boiling).

5. When ready to eat, carefully remove the lid using a towel or hot pads if the jar is still hot. Give the oats a good stir and top with a Frozen Whipped Cream Dollop.

> ### Tips
> - Use a mason jar jacket to make this a handheld, on-the-go breakfast.
> - A 6-quart pressure cooker will fit up to three pint-size jars, so increase the number of servings as needed
> - The oats cook more quickly and evenly with multiple jars in the pot. If only cooking a single serving, add 1–2 more jars (containing just water) inside the pot.

VARIATIONS

The ingredients listed in these variation recipes are meant to be added to the mason jar as the ½ cup of extras that the main recipe on page 23 calls for. Add garnishes after cooking is complete.

Peanut Butter Banana Oats

½ cup chopped bananas
1 tablespoon peanut butter
substitute maple syrup with 2 tablespoons of honey
garnish with Frozen Whipped Cream Dollop (page 189) and an extra drizzle of
    peanut butter (could substitute with almond butter if preferred)

Cherry Almond Pie Oats

½ cup halved cherries
2 tablespoons sliced or slivered almonds
¼ teaspoon almond extract
garnish with Frozen Whipped Cream Dollop (page 189) and extra sliced or
    slivered almonds

Apple Cinnamon Oats

½ cup diced apples
2 tablespoons golden raisins
¾ teaspoon cinnamon
garnish with Frozen Whipped Cream Dollop (page 189)

Carrot Cake Oats

½ cup finely shredded carrots
2 tablespoons raisins
¾ teaspoon cinnamon
¼ teaspoon pumpkin pie spice
garnish with Frozen Whipped Cream Dollop (page 189)

Chocolate Covered Strawberry Oats

½ cup chopped strawberries
1 tablespoon mini chocolate chips (semisweet or milk)
garnish with Frozen Whipped Cream Dollop (page 189) and a sprinkle of mini
   chocolate chips

Lemon Blueberry Oats

zest and juice of 1 lemon
½ cup blueberries
garnish with Frozen Whipped Cream Dollop (page 189) and extra blueberries.
optional: While the oatmeal is cooking, place 1 cup of frozen blueberries in
   a saucepan. Add 2 tablespoons of water and sprinkle with ½ teaspoon of
   cornstarch. Stir to combine. Bring to a boil, reduce heat, and simmer until
   thick and syrup-like. When oatmeal is done, stir the oats and then swirl in a
   scoop of the blueberry syrup.

Mini Frittatas

This egg dish has quickly become a big favorite around my house. Not only for the fact that this egg muffin turns out perfectly moist and fluffy every time, or that it takes seconds to throw together, or even that I can make them by using extra bits of vegetables, cheese, and meat that are waiting to be used from my fridge. Oh no, these are a favorite because—instead of me putting spinach, cheese, and ham in my kids' eggs—my kids can put spinach, cheese, and ham in their own personalized ramekin, and suddenly it's their idea, and it's a work of art. I wish I had known to take psychology classes more seriously in school. It really would have helped with motherhood! Eat them dipped in ketchup or hot sauce, wrapped up in a tortilla, or on a buttery, toasted English muffin. Limitless toppings, endless possibilities.

Prep: 10 minutes
Pressure: 8 minutes
Total: 25 minutes

Pressure: High
Release: 2-minute natural
Serves: 4–6

Ingredients

7 eggs
big pinch of kosher salt
coarse black pepper
toppings: ham, spinach, cheese (cheddar, feta, pepper jack),
    diced bell pepper, tomato, pesto, etc.

> For a thicker frittata, divide the batter between fewer ramekins and keep the same cooking time. I like to make a thicker egg and melt cheese over the top if I'm eating it on an English muffin.

Directions

1. Grease six 6-ounce ramekins with nonstick cooking spray and set aside. Prepare toppings (chop ham, shred cheese, chop spinach, etc.). Place in bowls or make piles of each on a cutting board.

2. Crack eggs into a bowl and beat well; season with salt and pepper.

3. Divide eggs evenly between ramekins (a large cookie scoop makes fast, clean work of this). Top eggs with desired toppings (this is where the kids have their fun), then give each ramekin a light stir.

4. Add 1 cup of water to the pressure cooker pot and place trivet inside. Place three ramekins on the trivet, top with a second trivet, and add the last three ramekins. Secure the lid and turn pressure release knob to a sealed position. Cook at high pressure for 8 minutes.

5. When cooking is complete, use a natural release for 2 minutes and then release any remaining pressure.

6. Carefully remove ramekins and serve warm, as is, with ketchup or hot sauce, or on a toasted, buttered English muffin.

Peach Melba Steel Cut Oats

I love sending my family out for the day with the long-lasting fuel that steel cut oats provide and not worrying that they'll get hungry and irritable before lunch time. Plus, between the oats and the chia seeds, this breakfast packs a major fiber punch, which is huge when dealing with the unpredictable diet of kids. This version gets major points around here for the two most important reasons: appearance and taste. Pops of orange and pink in a fountain of creamy white score high in the presentation department. Peaches get cooked along with the oats and transform into a thick peachy syrup. Combine that with tart-sweet raspberries and cream, and I'm gonna call that a 10 all day.

Prep: 5 minutes
Pressure: 10 minutes
Total: 30–40 minutes

Pressure Level: High
Release: 10-minute natural
Serves: About 6

Ingredients

1½ cups steel cut oats
5 cups water
½ cup pure maple syrup
pinch of salt
2 cups fresh or frozen peach slices
¼ cup chia seeds
1 cup fresh or frozen raspberries
Frozen Whipped Cream Dollops (page 189)

> I like to prep the oats the night before, by placing the oats, water, syrup, and salt in the pot. When I wake in the morning, I add the peaches and start the pressure cooker. After the cooking is complete, leave the oats in the pressure cooker with the lid in place. The oats stay nice and hot for at least a half hour, while everyone is getting ready. When it's time to eat, I stir in the chia seeds, top with raspberries, set the table, and pour milk while the chia seeds absorb some of the liquid.

Directions

1. Add oats, water, syrup, salt, and peaches to the pressure cooker pot and stir. Secure the lid and turn pressure release knob to a sealed position. Cook at high pressure for 10 minutes.

2. When cooking is complete, use a natural release for 10 minutes (can also use a full natural release if not in a hurry). If liquid sprays through valve, either place a towel over the top of the valve or turn back to the sealed position and allow to cool for 5–10 more minutes.

3. Sprinkle chia seeds over the top and stir in quickly so they don't clump together. Scatter the raspberries over the top and place the lid back on for 10 minutes to allow chia seeds to swell and raspberries to release some of their juices.

4. Serve hot with a Frozen Whipped Cream Dollop in the center.

Peaches and Cream Steel Cut Oats with Cinnamon Maple Drizzle

If I were of royal status and could have a steaming hot breakfast ready for me everyday after a hard morning run (because being royal doesn't mean you don't have to work for that beach body), this is what it would look like: a tower of soft, eggy French toast stuffed with warm, sweet peaches, a cascading waterfall of maple syrup, a fluffy cloud of vanilla whipped cream, and a sprinkle of cinnamon, all served on a white platter etched with pure gold . . . okay, back to reality. Since no one is cooking for me in the mornings, I created this: Peaches and Cream Steel Cut Oats with Cinnamon Maple Drizzle. It hits all the flavor notes I crave, plus it's quick, healthy, and will keep you energized for HOURS because—chia seeds! One teeny, tiny little seed that gives my family the fiber and protein they need to really take charge of a day.

Prep: 5 minutes
Pressure: 10 minutes
Total: 30-40 minutes

Pressure Level: High
Release: 10-minute natural
Serves: About 6

Ingredients
1½ cups steel cut oats
6 cups water
pinch of salt
Cinnamon Maple Drizzle
¼ cup chia seeds
Peach Compote (page 207)
Frozen Whipped Cream Dollops (page 189)

For Cinnamon Maple Drizzle
½ cup pure maple syrup
2 teaspoons cinnamon

Directions

1. Add oats, water, and salt to the pressure cooker pot and stir. Secure the lid and turn pressure release knob to a sealed position. Cook at high pressure for 10 minutes.

2. While oats are cooking, combine maple syrup and cinnamon in a small jar with a tight fitting lid and shake vigorously to combine. Set aside.

3. When pressure cooking is complete, use a natural release for 10 minutes (can also use a full natural release, if not in a hurry). If liquid sprays through the valve, turn back to a sealed position and allow to cool for 5-10 more minutes.

4. Sprinkle chia seeds over the top and stir in quickly so they don't clump together. Place the lid back on the pot and let sit for 5-10 minutes to allow chia seeds to swell.

5. To serve, warm the Peach Compote in the microwave or on the stove top until nice and hot. Scoop oatmeal into a bowl, top with a Frozen Whipped Cream Dollop, cover with Peach Compote, and then drizzle with Cinnamon Maple Drizzle.

Cherry Pineapple Upside-Down Steel Cut Oats

Steel cut oats are my number one favorite thing to make for my family in the mornings. Not only are they healthy and full of fiber and protein, they are a breeze to put together and are a one-pot meal on those crazy school mornings. So obviously, I make them often . . . maybe too often. My daughter expressed concerns that I'm not like the other moms and all she wants "is a bowl of cereal!" Oh, the drama. So to keep it enticing, I've gotta keep the flavors interesting. After my kids got to experience the heavenly wonders of a pineapple upside-down cake, I knew this had to be the next oatmeal flavor creation. And it was a HIT! No complaining that morning! Until she saw the PB and J on "brown" bread I packed in her lunch box . . . cue the different mom speech again.

Prep: 5 minutes
Pressure: 10 minutes
Total: 30–40 minutes

Pressure Level: High
Release: 10-minute natural
Serves: About 6

Ingredients

1½ cups steel cut oats
1 cup pineapple juice
5 cups water
¼ cup brown sugar
pinch of salt
1 cup chopped pineapple
¼ cup chia seeds
1 cup frozen cherries, chopped
Optional: cream or milk, extra brown sugar, sliced almonds

Directions

1. Add oats, pineapple juice, water, brown sugar, and salt to the pressure cooker pot and stir. Secure the lid and turn pressure release knob to the pressure position. Cook at high pressure for 10 minutes.

2. When cooking is complete, use a natural release for 10 minutes (can also use a full natural release, if not in a hurry) then release any remaining pressure. If liquid sprays through the valve, turn it back to a sealed position and allow to cool for 5–10 more minutes.

3. Add chopped pineapple and sprinkle chia seeds over the top; stir in quickly so the seeds don't clump together. Scatter chopped cherries over the top; do not stir in! As the cherries thaw, they will release their juices over the top of the oats. Place the lid back on the pot and let sit for 5–10 minutes to allow chia seeds to swell and cherries to thaw.

4. To serve, scoop oats into a bowl and top with a drizzle of cream or milk, extra brown sugar, and almonds, if desired.

Pumpkin Pecan Breakfast Cake with Maple Cinnamon Sauce

Given that breakfast cakes are my family's favorite morning meal and that I adore the taste and smell of pumpkin spice everything, this Pumpkin Pecan Breakfast Cake just had to be born. I created this heavenly version with pumpkin, cinnamon, cranberries, and pecans. The cake itself is mildly sweet, which I love, but my kids needed an extra sumpin' sumpin', so maple cinnamon drizzle made with yogurt to keep it breakfast-y, it is! If I'm feeling like I need some points in the "Best Mom Ever" department, I'll even swap out the cranberries for chocolate chips, which we can all agree is a very good choice!

Prep: 10 minutes
Pressure: 35 minutes
Total: 65 minutes

Pressure Level: High
Release: 10-minute natural
Serves: About 8

Ingredients

6 eggs
¼ cup brown sugar, lightly packed
3 tablespoons butter, melted
1½ cup pumpkin (can substitute Easy Pumpkin Butter from page 203)
1½ cup plain yogurt
2 teaspoons vanilla extract
1½ cups whole wheat pastry flour or white whole wheat flour
1 teaspoon salt
1 tablespoon baking powder
2 teaspoons cinnamon
1½ teaspoons pumpkin pie spice
¾ cup dried cranberries
¾ cup chopped pecans

For Maple Cinnamon Sauce

1 cup yogurt
¼ cup maple syrup
1 teaspoon cinnamon
½ teaspoon vanilla extract

Add an extra 15 minutes to the cook time if not using a heating core.

Directions

1. Grease a 7- or 8-inch springform pan or pushpan and the heating core with nonstick cooking spray (if using a 7-inch pan, it needs to be a true 7 inches in diameter and at least 3 inches tall).

2. Beat together the eggs and sugar until smooth. Add the butter and mix well. Add pumpkin, yogurt, and vanilla; whisk to combine.

3. In a separate bowl, whisk together the flour, salt, baking powder, cinnamon, and pumpkin spice. Combine with the egg mixture. Fold in the cranberries and pecans.

4. Place the heating core in the center of the prepared pan and fill with batter. Pour the remaining batter into the pan, making sure to keep the core in the center of the pan.

5. Add 1 cup of water to the pressure cooker pot and place a trivet inside. Carefully place the springform pan on the trivet. Secure the lid and turn pressure release knob to a sealed position. Cook at high pressure for 35 minutes.

6. While the cake is cooking, make the Maple Cinnamon Sauce. Add all of the sauce ingredients into a small bowl and whisk until smooth.

7. When pressure cooking is complete, use a 10-minute natural release.

8. Place the pan on a cooling rack and carefully remove the springform ring.

9. Serve the cake warm with a drizzle of Maple Cinnamon Sauce.

VEGETABLES

"Baked" Sweet Potato: Sweet or Savory

Pressure cookers are the perfect cooking environment for potatoes of every variety. Featured in this recipe are sweet potatoes. The moist conditions make sweet potatoes amazingly fluffy and, dare I say, melt-in-your-mouth creamy. Is that even a typical description for sweet potatoes? Enjoy it sweet, like my kids prefer, or savory, loaded with spinach and garbanzo beans. I know—strangest, most wonderful combination ever!

Prep: 2 minutes
Pressure: 25 minutes
Total: 30 minutes

Pressure Level: High
Release: Quick
Serves: About 4

Ingredients
2 large sweet potatoes

Directions

1. Pierce sweet potatoes a few times with a sharp pointed knife. Add 2 cups of water to the pressure cooker pot and place trivet inside. Place sweet potatoes on top of the trivet. Secure the lid and turn pressure release knob to a sealed position. Cook at high pressure for 25 minutes.

2. When cooking is complete, use a quick release. Poke the potatoes with a fork to make sure they are done; fork should slide through with ease. If more cooking is necessary, secure the lid and cook at high pressure for another 5 minutes.

Sweet variation: Cinnamon Sugar Sweet Potato

Butter to taste
Cinnamon and sugar to taste

Directions

1. When potatoes are ready, slit them lengthwise and put a couple pats of butter on top to melt. Sprinkle with cinnamon sugar.

Savory variation: Spinach and Garbanzo Bean Stuffed Sweet Potato

1 tablespoon butter
¼ cup chopped onion
4 cups fresh spinach, coarsely chopped
2 ounces whipped cream cheese
¼ cup light sour cream or plain yogurt
1 cup canned white beans, rinsed and lightly mashed
salt and pepper to taste
¼ cup shredded Monterey Jack cheese

Directions

1. While sweet potatoes are cooking, place butter in a sauté pan over medium heat. Add onions and cook until soft, about 3-4 minutes. Add spinach and toss in pan for 2-3 minutes until wilted. Remove from heat.

2. When sweet potatoes are cooked and cooled slightly, slice potatoes in half lengthwise and scrape about half of the sweet potato from its peel, leaving the peel intact and sturdy. Mash the sweet potato with cream cheese and sour cream or yogurt. Stir in white beans, spinach-and-onion mixture, and a big pinch of salt and pepper.

3. Divide the mixture between the four potato skins. Preheat oven broiler. Top with shredded cheese and set under the broiler to melt and brown the cheese, about 1-2 minutes. Serve hot.

For making Duchess Potatoes ahead, after potatoes have been piped onto the sheet pan, place in freezer until solid. Transfer to a sealable freezer bag. When ready to cook, simply place desired number of potatoes onto sheet pan, brush with melted butter, sprinkle with kosher salt, and cook as directed above. May need an extra 5 minutes cooking time.

Buttermilk and Chive Mashed Potatoes or Duchess Potatoes

Prior to owning an electric pressure cooker, the only thing I thought pressure cookers were used for was mashed potatoes because that's all I ever saw my mom use it for. Mashed potatoes are one of those foods that I feel like I've had enough times to keep me happy for life. But how could I not make mashed potatoes for my pressure cooker cookbook after believing for years that's all it was good for? Not only am I including my favorite mashed potato recipe, but a new, inventive way to make them fancy: Duchess Potatoes, or as my daughter calls them, Princess Potatoes.

Prep: 10 minutes
Pressure: 8–10 minutes
Total: 30 minutes

Pressure Level: High
Release: Quick
Serves: 6

Ingredients

3 pounds Yukon Gold potatoes, peeled and cubed
1 cup buttermilk
3 tablespoons butter
1¼ teaspoons salt
½ teaspoon pepper
¼ cup fresh chives, finely minced

Directions

1. Add 1 cup of water to the pressure cooker pot and place trivet inside. Place potatoes into a mesh steamer basket and place on the trivet (or use a collapsible steamer basket). Secure the lid and turn pressure release knob to a sealed position. Cook at high pressure for 8–10 minutes.

2. When cooking is complete, use a quick release. Poke the potatoes with a fork to make sure they are very tender. If they are still firm, replace the lid and cook for another 1–2 minutes at high pressure.

3. Place potatoes, buttermilk, butter, salt, and pepper in the bowl of a mixer with a whisk attachment. Mix at medium speed until smooth, being careful not to overmix (to prevent the potatoes from becoming gummy). Add chives and mix just until incorporated.

4. Alternatively, potatoes can be mashed using a ricer or potato masher. Serve warm.

Duchess Potatoes

3 egg yolks
melted butter or cooking spray
kosher salt

Directions

1. After potatoes have been mashed with buttermilk, butter, salt, and pepper, add 3 egg yolks to the mixer while it runs at low speed. Mix in chives.

2. Preheat oven to 425°F. Line two baking sheets with nonstick foil or parchment paper. Spoon potato mixture into a pastry bag, fitted with a large star tip. Pipe decorative mounds onto pan, about 2 inches in diameter and about 2 inches apart. Brush potatoes with melted butter or spray with cooking spray and sprinkle lightly with kosher salt. Bake 15–20 minutes until tops are lightly browned. Serve hot.

Corn on the Cob

My mom argues with me that the pressure cooker couldn't possibly make something like boiling corn on the cob any easier. But I 100% disagree. I throw the corn in, press a button, and walk away. No water splatters burning my arms, and there's no checking again and again wondering if it's done. It's just perfect at 4 minutes, every time.

Prep: 1 minute
Pressure: 4 minutes
Total: less than 10 minutes

Pressure Level: High
Release: Quick
Serves: 6-8

Ingredients

corn on the cob (6-8 cobs, however many will fit in the pot)
butter
salt
lemon pepper (if desired)

Directions

1. Add 1 cup of water to the pot of the pressure cooker and place a collapsible steamer basket or a trivet inside. Place desired number of cobs in the basket/trivet. Secure the lid and turn pressure release knob to a sealed position. Cook at high pressure for 4 minutes.

2. When cooking is complete, use a quick release.

3. Spread the cooked cobs with butter, and add a sprinkle of salt and lemon pepper.

> To caramelize corn, heat a skillet or grill to high heat. Add corn and rotate until some of the kernels are brown.

Creamy Pesto Vegetable Medley

When I first made this dish, it reminded me of one of the first meals I ate with my new family after I was married. My husband's family is "game on" when it comes to meat, but I could happily be vegetarian, if I had to. I remember panicking at a Sunday meal where everyone was oohing and ahhing over a plate full of perfectly rare steak. Keep in mind, I grew up being taught that, if I ate pink meat, I would surely die (mild exaggeration). With a quick scan of the table, I realized I could fill up on some delicious-looking cauliflower, broccoli, and carrots covered in cheese sauce. Worried about offending anyone, I put a small steak on my plate and created a barrier with mashed potatoes to keep what I thought was raw blood from touching the best veggies I'd ever eaten. My in-laws have since taught me how a properly cooked piece of meat should look and taste, but those cheesy veggies made by my rock-star mother-in-law still reign supreme for me. My mother-in-law is my kind of cook and is one of my favorite people to have eat my food. She just gets my unique style of cooking and makes me feel like a pro, even when something doesn't quite work out as I planned. So while not an exact replica of her cheesy vegetables I loved so much, these pesto veggies are an homage to the woman who raised my husband to be such a good man.

Prep: 2 minutes
Pressure: 1 minute
Total: 10 minutes

Pressure Level: High
Release: Quick
Serves: 4–6

Ingredients

12–16-ounce bag fresh broccoli, cauliflower, and carrot mix, prewashed
2 tablespoons whipped cream cheese
1 tablespoon milk (any kind)
1 tablespoon prepared basil pesto
kosher salt

> Broccoli and cauliflower cook faster than carrots in the pressure cooker. Putting the carrots directly in the water to cook will speed up their cooking time, so all of the vegetables are done at the same time.

Directions

1. Add 1 cup of water to the pressure cooker pot. Place only the carrots into the water. Place a collapsible steamer basket on top of the carrots. Add broccoli and cauliflower to basket. Secure the lid and turn pressure release knob to a sealed position. Cook at high pressure for 1 minute.

2. When cooking is complete, use a quick release. Holding the handle, remove the collapsible steamer basket from the pot. Drain water from the carrots and add them to the basket; set aside. Return pot to the pressure cooker, add cream cheese, milk, and pesto. Select sauté and whisk to combine ingredients. Add vegetables to the pot, sprinkle with a big pinch of kosher salt, and stir to coat with sauce. Stir gently so the vegetables don't mash. Serve warm.

Potatoes are a great base for many different flavors. Feel free to try a different combination of herbs and seasonings every time you make these!

Herbed Fingerling Potatoes

Fingerling potatoes instantly make me feel like I'm making something gourmet. They just look like expensive restaurant food, even if I'm covered in finger paint and glitter while eating them. My youngest sister Maegan introduced me to this dish, and it was an instant hit. Maegan shares my same love of cooking and actually owned a pressure cooker before I had even considered the purchase, so this recipe is for her. She lovingly watched my children during the hardest possible phase of twins and did it with grace and patience. She now has kids of her own and constantly impresses me with her skills as a hands-on mom. We have dreams of one day living together in a big ol' house where we could watch each other's kids on weekends and have endless amounts of incredible food. This also means we would have one heck of a gym. Dream big, right?

Prep: 5 minutes
Pressure: 6 minutes
Total: 20 minutes

Pressure Level: High
Release: Quick
Serves: 4-6

Ingredients

1½ pounds fingerling potatoes
¼ cup kosher salt
2 sprigs fresh rosemary
2 sprigs fresh thyme
2 cloves garlic, smashed
olive oil

Directions

1. Place potatoes in a mesh steamer basket and add to the pressure cooker pot. Add enough water to cover potatoes by 1 inch. Add salt, herbs, and garlic; stir. Secure the lid and turn pressure release knob to a sealed position. Cook at high pressure for 6 minutes.

2. When cooking is complete, use a quick release.

3. Lift mesh basket from the pressure cooker and discard garlic and herbs, as well as the water from the pot.

4. Serve potatoes hot with a side of Sour Cream and Chive Dip.

For Sour Cream and Chive Dip

½ cup sour cream
⅛ cup chopped chives

Directions for Sour Cream and Chive Dip

1. Stir together sour cream and chives.

Variation: Crispy Herbed Fingerling Potatoes

The potatoes are very flavorful as is, but are over the top when sautéed until brown and crispy. This can be done in two batches directly in the pressure cooker pot or in a single batch on the stove top in a large skillet.

Directions

1. After cooking, slice the potatoes in half, on a slant. Press sauté or brown on the pressure cooker and add enough olive oil to lightly coat the bottom of the pan (or in a skillet on the stove top: heat pan on high heat and add enough oil to lightly coat bottom). Place potatoes cut-side-down in the pan (or skillet) and don't move them for 1–2 minutes. You want them well browned but not burnt. When nice and crispy, remove from heat. Add an extra sprinkle of kosher salt and toss well.

Honey Glazed Carrots

Such a simple recipe, yet such an amazing game changer for carrots. I don't know why, but carrots carry a stigma as being "diet food" for me. I'm not sure where the thought comes from, but it's the reason carrots fall close to dead last on my preferred vegetable list . . . until now. Butter, honey, orange zest, and kosher salt compliment the carrot's natural sweetness perfectly and instead make them feel like a wonderful indulgence!

Prep: 1 minute
Pressure: 4 minutes
Total: 10 minutes

Pressure Level: High
Release: Quick
Serves: 4-6

Ingredients
1-pound bag baby carrots
1½ tablespoons butter
2 tablespoons honey
zest of 1 small orange
½ teaspoon kosher salt
chopped fresh parsley, for garnish

Directions

1. Add 1 cup of water to the pressure cooker pot. Add the carrots. Secure the lid and turn pressure release knob to a sealed position. Cook at high pressure for 4 minutes.

2. When cooking is complete, use a quick release.

3. Drain water from the pot. Push carrots to one side of the pot; to the empty space, add butter, honey, orange zest, and kosher salt to the pot. Using the sauté function, warm the ingredients and stir, until a smooth sauce develops. Stir carrots into the sauce until evenly coated.

4. Serve hot with a sprinkle of chopped parsley.

Easy, Healthy Tamales—2 ways:

Barbacoa Beef Tamales

Veggie and Goat Cheese Tamales

The first time I made tamales was when my husband and I were first married. I knew my husband loved them and I was still in the "must be perfect wife" phase. So I whipped up some tamales and sat at the edge of my seat as he tasted them. "Yum, really good," he replied. I tried them next and silently thought, "These are so dry. Why do people like tamales?" To keep my "perfect" status up, I made them again and again and smothered mine in sour cream so I could choke them down. Finally, one night, my husband said, "You don't need to make these; you can just buy them at the store." Which I immediately translated into, "These are disgusting, you can't cook, I can't believe I married someone that cooks such gross food" (remember, newlywed). So I never made them again . . . until now! And they are awesome! I know because I picked up some tamales from a Mexican food truck, made two recipes of my own, then laid out three tamales for my husband to try, and he picked MINE! Nailed it! Back to "Perfect Wife" status . . . except I stopped aiming for that three children ago.

Prep: 45 minutes
Pressure: 20 minutes
Total: 85 minutes

Pressure Level: High
Release: 10-minute natural
Serves: 6

Ingredients
about 16–18 dried corn husks
2½ cups drained, canned corn (can substitute fresh corn)
2 cups masa harina
½ cup warm chicken or vegetable broth
1 teaspoon baking powder
1 teaspoon kosher salt
4 tablespoons melted coconut oil

Toppings
Mexican crema, sour cream, or Greek yogurt
Tomatillo Avocado Salsa (next page)
crumbled Cotija cheese

For the Barbacoa Beef Tamales
shredded beef (page 55, steps 1-4)
pickled jalapeño rings
pepper jack cheese, cut into matchsticks

For the Veggie and Goat Cheese Tamales
½ cup diced roasted red pepper (homemade or from a jar)
½ cup drained, canned corn (can substitute fresh corn)
½ cup black beans, rinsed and drained
½ cup crumbled goat cheese

Directions

1. Fill a large bowl with warm water and place corn husks inside. Allow to soak and soften for 10–15 minutes.

2. To make masa dough: In a blender, add corn and pulse until partially pureed. Pour the corn into a large bowl and add masa harina, broth, baking powder, salt, and coconut oil. Use hands to combine all of the ingredients into a soft dough.

3. Drain corn husks and pat dry. Tear the small husks into ¼-inch strips for tying the tamales after they are filled. Lay several medium-large husks out on a clean surface. Scoop about 2-3 tablespoons of masa dough, flatten by hand, and place in the center of the top half of a corn husk. Use your fingers to spread the dough out onto the husk, leaving it about a ¼-inch thick.

4. For the Barbacoa Beef version: Arrange 1-2 tablespoons of shredded beef down the center of the dough. Place 3 jalapeño rings on top of the meat, followed by a matchstick of pepper jack.

5. For the Veggie version: Mix red pepper, corn, and black beans together in a small bowl. Add 2 tablespoons of mixture down the center of the dough followed by a sprinkle of crumbled goat cheese.

6. Fold over one long side of the corn husk so the dough encapsulates the filling. Fold over the other long side to overlap the other. Fold the triangle shaped bottom up so it lies over the filled portion of the tamale; and tie with the strips of corn husk.

7. Add 1 cup water to the pressure cooker pot and place a collapsible steamer basket inside (could also place a short trivet inside followed by an 8-inch perforated pan). Arrange tamales upright in the basket or pan (the open end should point up, the folded end should point down). Secure the lid and turn pressure release knob to a sealed position. Cook at high pressure for 20 minutes.

8. When cooking is complete, use a natural release for 10 minutes and then release any remaining pressure.

9. To serve, unroll tamales from the husk and arrange 2-3 on a plate. Top with Tomatillo Avocado Salsa, crema, and a sprinkle of Cotija cheese.

Tomatillo Avocado Salsa

½ pound tomatillos, husked, rinsed, and chopped
1 avocado, chopped
2 tablespoons diced onion
2 tablespoons chopped cilantro
1 jalapeño, membrane and seeds removed, minced
juice of 1 lime
½ teaspoon kosher salt, more to taste

Directions

1. Add the salsa ingredients to a small bowl and toss to combine. This can be made up to 3 days in advance by omitting the avocado and then adding it in right before serving.

To freeze tamales: Let them cool. Leave the tamales in the husk and place in gallon-sized resealable freezer bags. Place in the freezer. When ready to serve, pour 1 cup of water into the pressure cooker pot, followed by a steamer basket. Cook for 5 minutes at high pressure, followed by a 5-minute natural release. Dinner is served!

If you're in a hurry, simply place the meat and all of the sauce ingredients (unblended) into the pot of the pressure cooker. Browning the meat adds flavor, but this meat is still delicious without the extra step.

Barbacoa Beef Burritos
with Butternut Squash Nacho Cheese Sauce

One of my most favorite things to use the pressure cooker for is large batches of shredded meat. Shredded meat can be transformed into so many things, and then leftovers can be frozen for easy meals down the road. This barbacoa beef is knock-your-socks off flavorful, and this here burrito recipe is only one of many ways to enjoy it (see page 52 for Barbacoa Tamales!). I decided to roll this juicy meat up in a tortilla and call it a burrito, but when Cami came to take a picture of it, she took one look at it, and I knew by the awkward silence that I'd done something horribly wrong. "What?!" I inquired. "Where's the sauce?" "Does a burrito have to have sauce? I have salsa and sour cream." Again awkward silence, and I knew through sister telepathy, I had better come up with a sauce. In a panic, I scanned my fridge for the answer and beheld a mason jar of butternut squash cheese sauce. Its original purpose was to trick my kids into eating vegetables on their mac and cheese (they told me I needed to call Grandma for the blue box recipe), and since that didn't work, its second purpose was Ultimate Burrito. A little bit of this and a little bit of that, and we had nacho cheese sauce ready to pour all over the burrito to trick adults everywhere into smothering their burritos in vegetables.

Prep: 15 minutes
Pressure: 90 minutes
Total: About 2 hours

Pressure Level: High
Release: Natural
Serves: 6-8

Ingredients

½ medium onion
juice of 2 limes
⅓ cup apple cider vinegar
5 cloves garlic
2-3 chipotle chiles in adobo sauce (add more to make it spicier)
4 teaspoons cumin
1 tablespoon oregano
½ teaspoon ground cloves
1 tablespoon kosher salt
1 teaspoon pepper
½ cup beef broth

1 teaspoon oil
3-4 pound chuck or rump roast, visible fat removed, cut into 2-3 pieces
3 bay leaves
large whole grain tortillas
black beans, rinsed
Butternut Squash Nacho Cheese Sauce (page 171)
pepper jack cheese, grated
optional toppings: avocado, tomato, lettuce, sour cream, olives, hot sauce, guacamole, cilantro, pepper jack cheese, etc.

Directions

1. Add onion, lime juice, apple cider vinegar, garlic, chiles, cumin, oregano, cloves, salt, pepper, and beef broth to a blender and puree until smooth.

2. Add oil into the pressure cooker pot. Using the brown or sauté function, heat the oil until hot. Add meat and brown on all sides. Pour the sauce from the blender over the meat and add bay leaves. Secure the lid and turn pressure release knob to a sealed position. Cook at high pressure for 90 minutes.

3. When cooking is complete, use a natural release.

4. Place meat on a plate. Use two forks to shred it, then quickly return it to the pot.

5. Lay out a tortilla and top with a horizontal line of black beans and meat. Roll into a tight, open-ended burrito. Spoon Butternut Squash Nacho Cheese Sauce over the burrito followed by a sprinkle of grated pepper jack cheese. Broil to brown the cheese, if desired. Repeat for desired number of burritos. Serve hot with desired toppings.

To make this a one-pot dinner, wrap small- to medium-sized russet potatoes in tinfoil and set inside the middle of the uncooked ribs. The potatoes will be infused with the flavor of the ribs!

Barbecue Jerk Pork Ribs

I literally became a vegetarian (that didn't eat vegetables) as a kid when my brother revealed to me that my favorite fast food hamburger was made from a cow. Who knows why I had never realized it before, but the images that went through my head at that moment made it impossible for me to eat meat for quite some time. I counseled myself through that predicament until I witnessed someone eating ribs and my imagination wondered how a human could possibly eat meat off a bone. My husband has opened my eyes to many different foods, and the wonderful world of tender ribs is one of those foods. I still won't eat my ribs off the bone, but I will sit through lots of ridicule as I happily fork my meat from the bone. I just tell the teasers my daddy always told me I was a princess, and princesses don't stand for barbecue stains on their pretty faces. As for this recipe, I will never again make ribs any other way. Ribs were made for the pressure cooker, and what used to be something I made once a year, I will happily now make once a month.

Prep: 15 minutes
Pressure: 25-30 minutes
Total: 60-70 minutes
(plus 6-12 hours marinating time)

Pressure Level: High
Release: Natural
Serves: 6

For Jerk Marinade
2 tablespoons red wine vinegar
2 tablespoons brown sugar
1 tablespoon soy sauce
1 habanero, membrane and seeds removed
4 garlic cloves
2 green onions
1 inch fresh ginger, peeled
3 tablespoons freshly chopped cilantro
2 teaspoons smoked paprika
2 teaspoons salt
1 teaspoon ground allspice

1 teaspoon ground black pepper
1 teaspoon dried thyme
½ teaspoon cinnamon
¼ teaspoon ground cloves
¼ teaspoon ground coriander
2 tablespoons butter, melted

For Ribs
2 racks baby back pork ribs (about 2 pounds per rack)
½ cup apple juice
½ cup apple cider vinegar
Barbecue Sauce (page 169)

Directions

1. Place all Jerk Marinade ingredients into a blender or food processor. Pulse until mostly smooth.

2. Place each rack of ribs (bony side up) on a piece of tinfoil large enough to wrap the ribs completely. Remove the membrane from the bony side of the ribs if needed. Brush the marinade lightly over the bony side, then flip ribs over to brush the meaty side of the ribs with the remainder of the marinade. Wrap tightly with foil and allow to rest in the fridge 6 hours or overnight. (Ribs can be cooked immediately if needed, but will be more flavorful if allowed to marinate.)

3. Add apple juice and apple cider vinegar to the pressure cooker pot and place a short trivet inside. Remove ribs from the tinfoil and arrange the first rack of ribs vertically around the sides of the pot. Arrange the second rack vertically on the inside of the first rack. The racks can also be cut into 3 pieces each and placed inside the pot on top of a trivet (the pieces can be laid horizontally). Secure the lid and turn pressure release knob to a sealed position. Cook at high pressure for 25-30 minutes (depending on how large the racks are).

4. When cooking is complete, use a natural release.

5. Cover a baking sheet with foil and place ribs on top. Brush Barbecue Sauce generously over the ribs, leaving extra for serving and dipping. Place ribs under the oven broiler for 2-3 minutes or until the sauce starts to bubble and caramelize.

6. Cut between the bones to separate the individual ribs and serve with extra barbecue sauce for dipping.

Buffalo Chicken Stuffed Poblanos

I make a buffalo-stuffed jalapeño dish once or twice a year for big family get-togethers. It consistently turns spicy food avoiders into spicy food lovers. One Christmas, I took on the task without wearing gloves and my hands burned like fire for two days. Not only that, but stuffing that many little jalapeños is extremely tedious and really not something I look forward to. Then came this idea. Buffalo Chicken Stuffed Poblanos? Yes, Please! This is one of my husband's new favorite meals of the year, and it has already been requested for his birthday, alongside German Chocolate Cheesecake, (page 150), which I will so happily oblige.

Prep: 10 minutes
Pressure: 6 minutes
Total: 20 minutes

Pressure Level: High
Release: Quick
Serves: 3

Ingredients

⅓ cup hot sauce (like Frank's® RedHot Buffalo Wings Sauce)
2 cups cooked, shredded chicken
2 ribs celery, finely chopped
½ cup shredded Monterey Jack cheese, divided
½ cup blue cheese crumbles, divided
3 large poblanos, slit open, seeds and membrane removed

Directions

1. In a medium-sized bowl, add hot sauce, shredded chicken, celery, half of the Monterey Jack cheese, and half of the blue cheese. Toss to combine.

2. Stuff mixture into poblanos until it is slightly mounded (there may be filling left over depending on poblano size).

3. Add 1 cup of water to the pressure cooker pot and place trivet or 8-inch perforated pan inside. Place peppers on top of the trivet or pan. Secure the lid and turn pressure release knob to a sealed position. Cook at high pressure for 6 minutes.

4. When cooking is complete, use a quick release.

5. Preheat oven broiler, top peppers with remaining Monterey Jack and blue cheese. Place peppers under the broiler to melt and brown the cheese, about 1-2 minutes. Serve warm.

Pictured:
- Russet potatoes topped with chicken, cheddar, bacon, and chives and then placed under the broiler to melt the cheese.
- Sweet potato topped with chicken, Sour Cream and Chive sauce, blue cheese crumbles, and chopped celery.

Buffalo Chicken Stuffed Potatoes

Cami and I have been close sister friends our entire life, which shows just how well opposites can attract. Cami loves decorating and hates cooking. I adore cooking and have a panic attack in furniture and decor stores. She finds her peace on casual mountain hikes or walks on the beach. I find mine on fast-paced motorcycle adventures with my hubby. Even our kids are polar opposites! Mine can't comprehend sitting still or whispering, and hers are angels that always mind and talk polite (which she claims isn't true, but it mostly is). So when I told her of my buffalo-stuffed potato recipe, she insisted it be on a russet potato, while I felt a sweet potato was the only way to go. So we decided to embrace our differences, and offer up both variations to please a world built upon differing opinions. And I will do my very best not to gloat at the fact that, in the end, Cami did in fact decide my version was better.

Prep: 15 minutes
Pressure: 16 minutes
Total: 45 minutes

Pressure Level: High
Release: Natural
Serves: 6

Ingredients

1½ cups chicken broth
1 tablespoon smoked paprika
1½ teaspoons cumin
1½ teaspoons garlic powder
1½ teaspoons onion powder
1 teaspoon salt
½ teaspoon pepper
2½–3 pounds boneless, skinless chicken thighs
small- to medium-sized russet or sweet potato (about
    1 per person)
½–1 cup Frank's® RedHot Buffalo Wings Sauce
optional toppings: blue cheese crumbles, chopped
    celery, shredded sharp cheddar cheese, Sour
    Cream and Chive Sauce, bacon, minced chives

For Sour Cream and Chive Sauce

¾ cup sour cream (light or regular)
2 teaspoons minced chives
1 small garlic clove, minced
salt and pepper to taste

> Feel free to mix up toppings
> and type of potato as desired!

Directions

1. Pour chicken broth into the pressure cooker pot. Add paprika, cumin, garlic powder, onion powder, salt, and pepper; stir. Add chicken thighs and stir. Arrange chicken in a single layer on the bottom of the pan (or as close to a single layer as possible). Place a tall trivet on top of the chicken and arrange russet or sweet potatoes on top (no need to poke holes in the potatoes). Secure the lid and turn pressure release knob to a sealed position. Cook at high pressure for 16 minutes.

2. Meanwhile, whisk the Sour Cream and Chive Sauce ingredients together in a small bowl and set aside. (This sauce can be prepared up to 3 days in advance.)

3. When pressure cooking is complete, use a natural release.

4. Place potatoes on a plate and cover with foil to keep warm. Remove chicken from the pot and discard liquid. Place chicken in a bowl and shred. Pour Buffalo sauce over the chicken. Add more sauce to increase spice level as desired.

5. To serve, slice the potatoes longways and fluff (try not to shred the skin). Top with shredded buffalo chicken and desired toppings.

Caribbean Chicken Lettuce Wraps with Mango Citrus Dressing

This was a lot of different things before it came to be this recipe. A sandwich, a wrap, a big salad . . . all of which were good, but only good. *If I were to put the words "Caribbean," "mango," and "citrus" into one sentence, it needed to sing. I happened upon the cutest little baby romaine lettuce cups in my mom's fridge one day, and these miniature lettuce wraps were born. These mini lettuce wraps will dazzle and amaze at any get-together. Make an assembly line of lettuce cups, fill 'em, drizzle 'em, serve 'em, and watch people giggle with glee.*

Prep: 15 minutes
Pressure: 20 minutes
Total: 40 minutes (plus 2-4 hours marinating time)

Pressure Level: High
Release: Natural
Serves: 6-8

For Chicken
2 large chicken breasts
½ cup pineapple juice
¼ cup soy sauce
¼ cup scallions, chopped
½ jalapeño, membrane and seeds removed
2 tablespoons honey
juice of 2 limes
1 tablespoon Worcestershire sauce
1 clove garlic, minced
1 tablespoon grated fresh ginger
1 teaspoon curry powder
½ teaspoon ground coriander
½ teaspoon cayenne pepper
¼ teaspoon cinnamon
¼ teaspoon ground allspice

For Mango Citrus Dressing
1 large mango, peeled and pitted
¼ cup lime juice
¼ cup orange juice
2 tablespoons honey (can omit, if mango is very sweet)
½ teaspoon cumin
1 clove garlic
1 teaspoon salt
⅓ cup extra virgin olive oil
½ jalapeño, membranes and seeds removed, finely chopped
⅛ cup finely chopped cilantro
¼ teaspoon crushed red pepper flakes
freshly ground black pepper

To Assemble
baby romaine lettuce leaves or iceberg lettuce cups
1 red bell pepper, cored and diced
1 cup canned black beans, rinsed and drained
1 cup diced mango, pineapple, or mandarin oranges
1 cup diced jicama
fresh cilantro, chopped
sriracha

Directions

1. Add chicken breasts to a gallon-sized resealable bag. Add remaining ingredients for chicken to a blender and purée until smooth. Pour purée over the chicken breasts and toss to coat. Refrigerate for 2-4 hours.

2. Pour bag's contents into the pressure cooker pot. Secure the lid and turn pressure release knob to a sealed position. Cook at high pressure for 20 minutes.

3. While chicken is cooking, prepare the dressing by adding the mango, lime juice, orange juice, honey, cumin, garlic, and salt to a blender. Blend on low speed, drizzling in olive oil until combined and thick. Stir in jalapeño, cilantro, red pepper flakes, and black pepper. Taste and adjust the seasonings as desired.

4. When pressure cooking is complete, use a natural release.

5. Shred chicken inside pot with two forks.

6. **Put it together:** Line up desired number of lettuce cups. Fill with chicken, red bell pepper, black beans, diced mango (or pineapple or mandarin oranges), jicama, and cilantro. Drizzle with Mango Citrus Dressing and a few dots of sriracha. Serve immediately.

Don't stop at pasta with this dreamy sauce! Stir it into rice for a creamy cheesy rice, or use it as a dip for roasted veggies and warm crusty bread. Or if you really want to be dazzled, spread it on a pizza crust, top that with grilled chicken, bacon, Gorgonzola, mozzarella, and slices of tomatoes and then finish it off with a drizzle of balsamic after it's done cooking! It's heaven—it really is.

Cauliflower Fettuccine Alfredo

This Cauliflower Fettuccine Alfredo is a knock-off of my all-time favorite pasta dish at a very popular American Italian restaurant. While I loved that dish with my entire soul, I did not love the sick, heavy feeling that I felt each time I consumed all 1,300 calories and 70 grams of fat of it in one sitting. Ain't no morning run long enough to take care of that one. So to fulfill my need to have this dish often, I turned it into a big plate of vegetables starring the humble cauliflower. My family loves this pasta and few things make me happier than watching my kids happily devour a big plate of veggies. You could get even more crazy and substitute the pasta with spiralized zucchini, sweet potatoes, or butternut squash, but whatever you do, DO NOT nix that sweet balsamic drizzle. Then go right on ahead and guiltlessly lick your plate because this, my friends, is that good, and that good for you.

Prep: 10 minutes
Pressure: 6 minutes
Total: 30 minutes

Pressure Level: High
Release: 10-minute natural
Serves: 6

Ingredients

2 tablespoons butter
2 cloves garlic
7–8 cups cauliflower florets
1 cup chicken or vegetable broth
2 teaspoons salt
1 pound fettuccine pasta, preferably whole grain
2 cups spinach, coarsely chopped
2 green onions, finely chopped

For Garnish

Gorgonzola cheese, crumbled
sun-dried tomatoes, chopped
balsamic glaze or thick balsamic vinegar

> The sauce heats back up very nicely so you can make the sauce in advance and have it ready to pour over pasta for a quick, healthy, delicious meal any night of the week.

Directions

1. Select sauté on the pressure cooker and add butter. When melted, add garlic cloves and sauté until fragrant, about 2 minutes, stirring constantly so the garlic doesn't burn. Add cauliflower, broth, and salt. Secure the lid and turn pressure release knob to a sealed position. Cook at high pressure for 6 minutes.

2. While the cauliflower is cooking, heat a pot of water to boiling on the stove top. Add pasta and cook until al dente. Reserve about 1 cup of water and then drain the pasta. Return pasta to the empty pot.

3. When pressure cooking is complete, use a natural release for 10 minutes and then release any remaining pressure.

4. Blend with an immersion blender right in the pot until very smooth or carefully transfer to a blender and puree until smooth. With a spoon, stir in the chopped spinach and green onions and allow the hot sauce to wilt the spinach.

5. Pour sauce over the pasta and toss. If sauce is too thick, add a half cup or so of the reserved pasta water to thin as desired. The starchy water will help the sauce to stick to the pasta.

6. Serve hot with a garnish of crumbled Gorgonzola cheese, sun-dried tomatoes, and a drizzle of balsamic glaze (or vinegar).

Use canned white beans to thicken soups and sauces! Simply add some of the liquid from the pot into a blender and add ½–1 cup of rinsed and drained canned white beans, then blend until smooth. Stir the puree back into your pot of food. No cream needed!

Chicken Tikka Masala

I can't ever see a dish of Chicken Tikka Masala without recalling my first experience at an Indian cuisine restaurant. I like spicy food and never hesitate to ask for maximum spice level. So when they asked me how spicy on a scale of 1–5, I bravely requested the 5. I have never in my life had such spicy food. Within two bites, I tasted nothing, and my chest and stomach burned like fire. I tried taming it with rice, with naan, with cream, but it was basically inedible. "How is the food?" the kind waitress asked. And with a tear-streaked, flushed face, I whispered, "Amazing" . . . as she sweetly pretended not to notice my discomfort and handed me another cup of ice water. This pressure cooker Chicken Tikka Masala is bursting with flavor and spicy with warm Indian spices and won't require a three-day recovery; just as it was meant to be.

Prep: 15 minutes
Pressure: 9 minutes
Total: 40 minutes

Pressure Level: High
Release: 10-minute natural
Serves: 6

Ingredients

2 teaspoons oil
1 cup diced onion
1 jalapeño, minced, membrane and seeds removed
  for less spice
3 cloves garlic, minced
1 inch piece of fresh ginger, grated
28-ounce can tomato puree
juice of 1 lemon
1½ tablespoons garam masala
2 teaspoons smoked paprika

½ teaspoon cayenne pepper
¼ teaspoon turmeric
½ teaspoon curry powder
2 teaspoons kosher salt
1½ pounds boneless, skinless chicken thighs
½–1 cup lite coconut milk
salt and pepper
serve with: brown rice or whole grain naan; steamed
  broccoli or asparagus
garnish: Greek yogurt, roasted cashews, cilantro

Directions

1. Select sauté on the pressure cooker and add oil. When hot, add onions, jalapeño, garlic, and ginger; sauté until soft, about 4 minutes. Add tomato puree, lemon juice, garam masala, paprika, cayenne pepper, turmeric, curry powder, and salt; whisk to combine. Add chicken thighs and toss to coat the chicken. Secure the lid and turn pressure release knob to a sealed position. Cook at high pressure for 9 minutes.

2. When cooking is complete, use a natural release for 10 minutes and then release any remaining pressure (could also use a full natural release).

3. Remove chicken with a slotted spoon and place on a cutting board. Shred or cut chicken into bite-sized pieces. Cover with foil to keep warm.

4. Pour coconut milk into the pot with the sauce and blend with an immersion blender right in the pot until very smooth, or carefully pour coconut milk and sauce into a blender and puree until smooth. Optional: Select sauté and allow the sauce to simmer if a thicker consistency is desired.

5. Add chicken back into the sauce and stir to combine. Season with salt and pepper if needed.

6. Serve hot with brown rice or whole grain naan and a side of steamed broccoli or asparagus. Garnish with Greek yogurt, cashews, and chopped cilantro.

Brining is key to moist, flavorful chicken. For even more intense flavor, after the chicken is cooked, empty the pressure cooker, add 1 tablespoon of olive oil, and select the brown or sauté function. When hot, add chicken and brown well on both sides.

Chicken with Cheesy Herb Sauce on Rice

I don't know why I struggle so much to make a perfectly juicy piece of chicken, but I do, and it drives me crazy. Even cooking my chicken in broth in the bottom of the pressure cooker didn't seem quite right. It shredded great, but I wanted a juicy, browned, skillet-like version, and then . . . a light went on. I brined the chicken breasts for ultimate flavor and juiciness and cooked it above the pot's liquid; after the chicken was cooked, I emptied the pot, used the sauté feature to get some oil nice and hot, and then quickly seared my chicken to browned perfection. Finally, I had a thick and juicy restaurant-style chicken breast that I joyfully smothered in cheese sauce!

Prep: 10 minutes
Pressure: 10 minutes
Total: 30 minutes (plus 4-6 hours brining time)

Pressure Level: High
Release: Natural
Serves: 4

For Chicken
1 quart warm water
1/4 cup kosher salt
4 large boneless, skinless chicken breasts, trimmed
1 teaspoon kosher salt
½ teaspoon freshly cracked black pepper
½ teaspoon garlic powder
½ teaspoon paprika

For Cheesy Herb Sauce
5 ounces spreadable herb cheese (like Boursin)
¼ cup chicken broth
juice of 1 lemon
1 tablespoon chopped fresh basil
1 tablespoon chopped fresh chives

For Rice
1 cup long grain white rice
1½ cups chicken broth

Directions

1. To prepare the brine, place a gallon-sized resealable bag inside a bowl and pour in 1 quart of lukewarm water and ¼ cup kosher salt. Seal shut and gently shake to dissolve salt. Chill the bag of water and then add chicken. Place the bag in the fridge, in a bowl, in case the bag leaks. Brine the chicken for 4-6 hours (even an hour will work). Remove the chicken from the brine and pat dry with a paper towel.

2. In a small bowl, combine salt, pepper, garlic powder, and paprika; sprinkle over both sides of the chicken.

3. Add 1 cup of water to the pressure cooker pot. My suggested method of stacking is as follows: trivet, 8-inch perforated pan, two chicken breasts, trivet, two more chicken breasts (make sure there is space between the chicken breasts). Secure the lid and turn pressure release knob to a sealed position. Cook at high pressure for 10 minutes.

4. While chicken cooks, prepare the Cheesy Herb Sauce. Combine herb cheese, chicken broth, and lemon juice in a saucepan. Bring to a simmer over medium heat on the stove top. Add more broth if a thinner sauce is desired. Take off the heat and stir in basil and chives. Place lid on top to keep warm.

5. When pressure cooking is complete, use a natural release. Remove chicken onto a plate and cover with foil to keep warm.

6. Rinse out the pot; add the rice and chicken broth. Secure the lid and turn pressure release knob to a sealed position. Cook at high pressure for 3 minutes.

7. When cooking is complete, use a natural release for 10 minutes and then release any remaining pressure. Fluff rice with a fork.

8. To serve, slice chicken and place on a bed of rice. Drizzle the whole dish with plenty of cheese sauce.

If you have the luxury of two pressure cookers, cook the rice and chicken at the same time.

Curry Coconut Lime Chicken Tenders

Whenever Cami invites family over for Sunday dinner, my first thought is, "Hmm, is her husband going to make the Curry Lime Chicken? How can I politely insist that he make it? Would that be rude? Or since it's family, is that acceptable?" So many questions, but a very serious matter nonetheless. This is the most flavorful chicken I have ever tasted. Each bite is a journey as your taste buds light up with layers upon layers of flavor . . . all in one little piece of chicken. How is it possible!? Well, now I can make it for myself in my own home, and while it's not quite as good as when my brother-in-law makes it while I sit and have much-needed girl talk, it still takes my breath away every time. Combine it with the Sweet Curry Coconut Cashew Rice from page 121, and trust me, it's a match made in heaven.

Prep: 10 minutes	**Pressure Level:** High
Pressure: 5 minutes	**Release:** Natural
Total: 20 minutes	**Serves:** 4-6
(plus 8–12 hours marinating time)	

Ingredients

3 tablespoons oil
zest of 2 limes
2 teaspoons ground cumin
1 tablespoon ground coriander
4 tablespoons soy sauce
1 tablespoon kosher salt
4 tablespoons sugar
4 teaspoons curry powder
1 cup lite coconut milk

¼ teaspoon cayenne
1 small jalapeño, minced, membrane and seeds
    removed for less spice
2 pounds chicken tenders
1 tablespoon water
1 tablespoon cornstarch
fresh limes, cut into wedges
chopped pineapple

Directions

1. Combine oil, lime zest, cumin, coriander, soy sauce, salt, sugar, curry powder, coconut milk, cayenne, and minced jalapeño in a gallon-sized resealable plastic bag. Shake to combine ingredients, then add chicken tenders. Allow to marinate overnight.

2. After marinating, pour the bag's contents into the pressure cooker pot. Secure the lid and turn pressure release knob to a sealed position. Cook at high pressure for 5 minutes.

3. When cooking is complete, use a natural release.

4. Remove chicken, leaving the sauce in the pot. Use the sauté function to bring the mixture to a boil; simmer to intensify flavors. To make a thicker sauce, combine water and cornstarch; add to mixture, stirring constantly, until it thickens.

5. Return chicken to pot; stir. Serve chicken with an extra drizzle of sauce, a squeeze of fresh lime juice, and chunks of fresh pineapple.

Serve chicken with rice to soak up all the delicious flavors of the sauce. Go heavy with the lime juice to add a tangy zip to the entire dish.

Garlic Lemon Chicken Sandwich with Tangy Pickle Dressing

This is it: my favorite sandwich of all time. I really don't need to say anything more than that, but doesn't my favorite sandwich of all time deserve a little more of an intro? This toasty warm ciabatta roll is smeared with avocado on one side, tangy dressing packed with chopped pickles on the other, topped with provolone, bacon, and tomato. Yep, favorite sandwich of all time. 'Nuff said.

. . . .

Prep: 15 minutes
Pressure: 8 minutes
Total: 30 minutes
(plus 2–8 hours marinating time)

Pressure Level: High
Release: Natural
Serves: 4

. . . .

For Tangy Pickle Dressing
¼ cup mayo
¼ cup light sour cream
¼ teaspoon dried dill
½ teaspoon dried parsley
½ tablespoon finely minced onion
2 tablespoons finely minced dill pickle
pinch of kosher salt
juice of half a lemon

For Chicken
3 tablespoons of extra virgin olive oil
zest of 1 large lemon
3 cloves garlic, minced
2 teaspoons dried parsley
1 teaspoon kosher salt
½ teaspoon pepper
4 small boneless, skinless chicken breasts, trimmed
  and pounded thin
additional kosher salt
lemon pepper

For the Sandwich
butter
4 ciabatta rolls
4 slices provolone cheese
1 avocado, sliced and seasoned with salt and pepper
1 tomato, sliced and seasoned with salt and pepper
iceberg lettuce
8 slices bacon, cooked

Directions

1. **To make the dressing:** Mix all dressing ingredients in a small bowl and stir well to combine. This becomes even more flavorful with time. Can be prepared up to 4 days in advance.

2. **To make the chicken:** Add extra virgin olive oil, lemon zest, garlic, parsley, salt, and pepper to a gallon-sized resealable bag. Squeeze bag to mix ingredients together. Add chicken and coat with oil mixture. Allow to marinate up to 8 hours (can be done in 2 hours if needed).

3. Remove chicken from marinade; season with kosher salt and lemon pepper to taste.

4. Add 1 cup of water to the pressure cooker pot. My suggested method of stacking is as follows: trivet, 8-inch perforated pan, two chicken breasts, trivet, two more chicken breasts (make sure there is space between the chicken). Secure the lid and turn pressure release knob to a sealed position. Cook at high pressure for 8 minutes.

5. When cooking is complete, use a natural release.

6. **To assemble:** Butter inside of ciabatta rolls and broil in the oven until lightly browned. Slather the bottom roll with pickle dressing. Add chicken and a slice of provolone cheese and place under the broiler again to melt cheese. Top with avocado, tomato, lettuce, bacon, and the other half of the roll.

Ground Turkey Taco Salad

Something happened when I was pregnant with my twin boys. I became EXTREMELY sensitive to smells. So much so that I had to take food to my mom's, have her cook it, and then bring it back to my house to eat it. Somehow this obsession with strong smells stayed after my boys were delivered, and to this day, the smell of meat in my home really bothers me. The two things that have saved me from becoming a vegetarian (and ultimately from my husband never speaking to me again) are my grill and my pressure cooker. I was ecstatic when I threw a pound of ground turkey into my pressure cooker outside, to discover it came out even more flavorful and juicy than if I had done it in a skillet on my stove top. I get to leave the smell outside, all while enjoying one of my favorite meals ever: a taco salad. Or perhaps my favorite meal ever is actually guacamole with a side of taco salad . . . whatever.

Prep: 5 minutes
Pressure: 15 minutes
Total: 35 minutes

Pressure Level: High
Release: 10-minute natural
Serves: 4–6

Ingredients
1 pound ground turkey (or beef)
2 tablespoons dried onions
10–16-ounce bag shredded coleslaw
Taco Seasoning
8-ounce can tomato sauce
taco salad shells (store bought)
Toppings: guacamole, salsa, tomatoes, olives,
   avocado, shredded cheese, crushed tortilla chips,
   sour cream, ranch, hot sauce, etc.

For the Taco Seasoning
1 tablespoon chili powder
1 teaspoon cumin
1 teaspoon salt
¼ teaspoon paprika
¼ teaspoon pepper
⅛ teaspoon garlic powder
⅛ teaspoon onion powder
¼ teaspoon crushed red pepper flakes
⅛ teaspoon dried oregano

Directions

1. Add 1 cup of water to the pressure cooker pot and place trivet inside. Place 8-inch perforated pan on top of trivet and place ground meat on top (no need to crumble, just leave in one piece). A collapsible steamer basket or a trivet with a small grid would also work (you don't want your meat and veggies to fall through the holes). Sprinkle onions on top of the meat. Top with coleslaw. Secure the lid and turn pressure release knob to a sealed position. Cook at high pressure for 15 minutes.

2. While meat is cooking, mix together Taco Seasoning ingredients in a small bowl and set aside.

3. When pressure cooking is complete, use a natural release for 10 minutes and then release any remaining pressure.

4. Remove pan containing meat and coleslaw from the pot and set aside. Discard juices from inside the pot. Add can of tomato sauce and Taco Seasoning into the pressure cooker pot and stir well to combine. Return meat and coleslaw to the pot; select sauté. Use spoon to break up and stir to combine all of the ingredients until warmed through.

5. To serve, scoop meat into the taco salad shells and garnish with desired toppings.

This recipe can also be made using one pound of frozen meat. Cook the meat for 25 minutes instead of 15.

As long as your pan is leak-proof, this can be prepared a day or two in advance.

Italian Sausage Lasagna

For this recipe, I had several critics ask, "Why make lasagna in a pressure cooker?" And honestly, I don't have a perfect reason, but here are a few. Because my oven is number 2 since electric pressure cookers entered my life; it's a little bit faster; it won't heat up the kitchen; if I neglect it, it won't burn; it's delicious; and most importantly, because I can. This lasagna isn't labor intensive at all yet it is bursting with fresh tomato and basil flavors. I've also made it without sausage, and it is equally delicious. I honestly prefer it with a single instead of double layer of noodles, but my husband and children disagreed so strongly, that I left the recipe as it was. This can be assembled the day before and, after it's cooked, can be frozen for an easy freezer meal.

Prep: 20 minutes
Pressure: 20 minutes
Total: 60 minutes

Pressure Level: High
Release: 10-minute natural
Serves: 6

Ingredients

oil
1 pound turkey or pork bulk Italian sausage
2 cups ricotta cheese
1 cup chopped spinach
1½ cups shredded quesadilla cheese (can substitute mozzarella), divided
½ cup freshly grated Parmesan cheese
1 egg

1 teaspoon kosher salt
½ teaspoon pepper
¼ cup chopped fresh basil
25 ounces marinara sauce (like Mezzetta® Napa Valley homemade marinara)
8 ounces no-boil lasagna noodles, whole wheat preferred

Directions

1. Select brown or sauté on the pressure cooker and add oil. When hot, add sausage. Brown and crumble the meat until it's cooked through. Remove to a plate lined with paper towels to absorb the extra grease.

2. In a medium bowl, mix ricotta, chopped spinach, 1 cup quesadilla cheese, Parmesan cheese, egg, salt, pepper, and basil.

3. Lightly spray an 8-inch pushpan or springform pan with nonstick cooking spray. Spread about ½ cup sauce in the bottom of the pan. Top with a double layer of noodles (break the noodles to fit). Spread one third of the ricotta mixture over the noodles; sprinkle with a third of the sausage. Repeat the layers two more times, ending with a layer of sauce. (From bottom to top, you should have: sauce, noodles, cheese, sausage, sauce, noodles, cheese, sausage, sauce, noodles, cheese, sausage, and sauce.)

4. Add 1 cup of water to the pressure cooker pot and place trivet inside. Place the lasagna on the trivet using a silicone or tinfoil sling for easier removal. Secure the lid and turn pressure release knob to a sealed position. Cook at high pressure for 20 minutes.

5. When cooking is complete, use a natural release for 10 minutes and then release any remaining pressure.

6. Carefully remove the hot lasagna. Top with remaining ½ cup of quesadilla cheese (or mozzarella). Place under the oven broiler to brown the cheese. Allow the lasagna to rest and cool for 20 minutes before serving.

> The sides of the pan can be removed for slicing and serving (and the layered look sitting on a pretty platter is delightful!), but keeping the pan together makes the cutting process a bit cleaner.

> This needs an 8-inch pan in order to fit all of the ingredients. A 7-inch pan can only fit two layers (not the three layers written in the recipe), so if a 7-inch is all you have, make a mini lasagna with the extra ingredients for another day.

Maple Mustard Pork Tenderloin

For those who fear I made a serious goof on this recipe, the pressure cook time for this meat is indeed 3-4 minutes. I've overcooked pork tenderloin many times due to a mother that imbedded in my childhood brain that pink meant poisonous. Which may also be why I believed that meat meant dry and chewy. Pork tenderloin is one of my favorite cuts of meat when cooked to a slightly pink 145°F and when flavored with this amazing maple mustard marinade. And I couldn't help but giggle inside when my mom put her slice in the microwave until it was gray and tough, despite my Google search revealing that 145°F was indeed safe.

Prep: 10 minutes
Pressure: 3-4 minutes
Total: 25 minutes (plus overnight marinade)

Pressure Level: High
Release: Natural
Serves: 4-6

Ingredients
2 (12-16 ounces each) pork tenderloins, trimmed
salt and pepper
oil

For Marinade
⅓ cup maple syrup
¼ cup Dijon mustard
2 tablespoons soy sauce
2 tablespoons apple cider vinegar
kosher salt
black pepper

Directions

1. In a gallon sized resealable bag, add maple syrup, mustard, soy sauce, apple cider vinegar, and a generous pinch of salt and pepper. Seal bag shut and shake to combine ingredients. Place the pork tenderloins inside and seal the bag. Set bag inside a shallow container, making sure all of the pork is lying in the marinade. Allow to marinate in the fridge for at least 4 hours or overnight.

2. Add oil into the pressure cooker pot. Using the brown or sauté function, heat the oil until hot. Remove the tenderloins from the marinade (do not discard marinade; this will be your cooking liquid). Season the tenderloins with salt and pepper; add one at a time to the pot and brown on two sides. Pour pork marinade into the pot with the meat and scrape up any browned bits from the bottom of the pot.

3. Secure the lid and turn pressure release knob to a sealed position. Cook at high pressure for 3 minutes (4 minutes for larger tenderloins).

4. When cooking is complete, use a natural release.

5. Check the meat temperature to make sure the center is at least 145°F. (If not at 145°F, cook for 1-2 more minutes at high pressure, then quick release and again check internal meat temperature.)

6. Remove tenderloins from the pot and place on a cutting board to rest. Press sauté and simmer marinade until it thickens. Could also make a cornstarch slurry of 2 tablespoons water and 1 tablespoon of cornstarch and add that to the simmering liquid to thicken; stir constantly until desired consistency is reached.

7. Slice the tenderloins. Serve over rice with a drizzle of the thickened marinade.

Meatballs in Tomato Basil Marinara

I've never met a meatball that I didn't like, but the thought of them spattering oil all over my stove top has always kept me from making them. Pressure cooker to the rescue once again. Not only do these meatballs need not be pan-fried, but they are moist and incredibly tender, and freeze like a dream. Serve them over pasta, in a sub, or as I instruct with this recipe, with a large crusty bread spoon! Bonus points for making that a garlic butter-coated bread spoon.

Prep: 15 minutes
Pressure: 5 minutes
Total: 40 minutes

Pressure Level: High
Release: 10-minute natural
Serves: 6

Ingredients
½ cup whole wheat panko breadcrumbs
¼ cup milk
1 pound lean ground beef
1 pound lean ground turkey
¼ cup finely chopped pancetta or bacon
½ cup freshly grated Parmesan cheese
1 egg
1 teaspoon dried parsley
3 cloves garlic, minced
2 teaspoons dried onion flakes
1 teaspoon dried oregano
½ teaspoon fennel seeds, crushed by hand
½ teaspoon crushed red pepper flakes
2 teaspoons kosher salt
1 teaspoon pepper
additional freshly grated Parmesan cheese, for serving
warm crusty bread, for serving

For Sauce
1 teaspoon oil
2 cloves garlic, crushed
½ cup water or chicken broth
28-ounce can tomato puree
28-ounce can whole peeled tomatoes
2 teaspoons kosher salt
½ cup fresh basil leaves, torn

Directions

1. In a large mixing bowl, combine panko and milk. Add ground meat, pancetta (or bacon), Parmesan, egg, parsley, garlic, onion flakes, oregano, fennel, red pepper flakes, salt, and pepper. Gently mix by hand until combined. Using a cookie scoop, form meat into loose balls, about 2-3 tablespoons each. Set aside on a piece of foil.

2. To make sauce: Select sauté on the pressure cooker and add oil. When hot, add garlic and stir until aromatic, about 1 minute. Add water (or broth), tomato puree, and whole peeled tomatoes. Sprinkle with salt and scatter basil leaves on top. Do not stir. Arrange meatballs in circular pattern on top of the sauce. Secure the lid and turn pressure release knob to a sealed position. Cook at high pressure for 5 minutes.

3. When cooking is complete, use a natural release for 10 minutes and then release any remaining pressure.

4. Give the meatballs a good stir. If a thicker sauce is preferred, use the sauté function to simmer the sauce until thickened.

5. Serve hot with sprinkle of Parmesan and a piece of crusty bread for soaking up the sauce.

> Use leftover meatballs to make meatball subs. Simply brown a whole wheat hoagie roll and arrange meatballs and provolone cheese inside. Broil to melt cheese. Leftover meatballs also freeze wonderfully.

Mexican Stuffed Bell Peppers with Chipotle Lime Sauce

One of my husband's favorite dishes that I make is a sausage-stuffed bell pepper, topped with a homemade marinara sauce. Unfortunately, I have a problem. I don't get excited about making the same recipe twice, and it makes my husband crazy. He's even resorted to reverse psychology by saying, "Marci, this is gross, don't ever make it again." Well I'm not five, I know what he's doing, so what do I do? I agree to make a stuffed bell pepper and then promise him it'll be even better than the last one. To which he responds, "So if it's better, will you make it again?" To which I reply, "Yeah, of course" while very immaturely crossing my fingers behind my back. These peppers are definitely better because: one, there's absolutely no precooking required; two, the toppings, soooo many toppings; and three, four, and five—the Chipotle Lime Sauce.

Prep: 10 minutes
Pressure: 15 minutes
Total: 40 minutes

Pressure Level: High
Release: 10-minute natural
Serves: 4–6

Ingredients

1 pound lean ground turkey
4½-ounce can mild chopped green chiles
2 green onions, finely chopped
1 jalapeño pepper, seeded and diced
½ cup whole wheat panko (or other breadcrumbs)
2 teaspoons ground chili powder
1 teaspoon ground cumin
1 teaspoon garlic powder
1 teaspoon kosher salt
4 slices pepper jack cheese
4 bell peppers, tops, seeds, and membranes
   removed
Garnish: pico de gallo, chopped avocado, pickled
   jalapeños, crushed tortilla chips, and Chipotle Lime
   Sauce

For Chipotle Lime Sauce

½ cup light sour cream
1-2 tablespoons chipotle in adobo sauce
zest and juice of 1 lime
⅛ teaspoon garlic powder

Directions

1. To make the Chipotle Lime Sauce: In a small bowl, whisk to combine sour cream, chipotle in adobo sauce (just the sauce, not the peppers), lime zest and juice, and garlic powder. Store in refrigerator until ready to use. (Can be prepared up to 4 days in advance.)

2. In a large bowl, combine the ground turkey, green chiles, green onions, jalapeño, panko (or other breadcrumbs), chili powder, cumin, garlic powder, and salt. Stuff one-fourth of the mixture into each prepared bell pepper.

3. Add 1 cup of water to the pressure cooker pot and place trivet inside. Arrange peppers on the trivet. An 8-inch perforated pan also works well for this.

4. Secure the lid and turn pressure release knob to a sealed position. Cook at high pressure for 15 minutes. When cooking is complete, use a natural release for 10 minutes and then release any remaining pressure.

5. Preheat broiler. Place bell peppers on a baking sheet. Top with pepper jack cheese and broil until browned and bubbly.

6. To serve: Pile on pico de gallo, chopped avocado, pickled jalapeños, and some crushed tortilla chips. Finally, drizzle (or drown) it in the Chipotle Lime Sauce. Enjoy!

> Because the meat is raw to begin with, a lot of juices will collect inside the pepper while cooking. Either drain off the juices after cooking or, with a skewer, poke a hole in the bottom of the pepper before cooking.

Mongolian Beef with Quick Pickled Vegetables

Being an extremely routine person, I tend to order the same things at restaurants and have never had Mongolian beef. It was my mom, who orders Mongolian beef regularly at Chinese restaurants, who requested this meal. Many of the recipes I researched had more sugar than a standard cookie recipe, and I almost nixed the idea. But I wanted to make mama happy, so I went for it and cut the sugar WAY down, and guess what: my mom said it was the best she's ever had. Cue my face beaming. I took a small spin from the traditional presentation and set it aside brown rice noodles and my favorite pickled veggie trio. With this easy recipe in my recipe book, I will happily stay in my routine ways and order the ol' standby—Tiny Spicy Chicken—forever.

Prep: 15 minutes
Pressure: 10 minutes
Total: 40 minutes

Pressure Level: High
Release: Natural
Serves: 4

Ingredients

½ cup soy sauce
½ cup water
2 tablespoons honey (can substitute with Sweet Heat Infused Honey from page 221)
2 tablespoons brown sugar (optional for added sweetness)
1–3 teaspoons sriracha
2 garlic cloves, minced
1-inch knob of fresh ginger, grated
1 pound thinly sliced flank steak
2 tablespoons cornstarch
1 tablespoon oil
8-ounce package brown rice noodles

For Pickled Vegetables

1 cucumber, cut into matchsticks or spiralized
1 red bell pepper, cut into matchsticks or spiralized
1 carrot, cut into matchsticks or spiralized
¼ cup rice vinegar
2 teaspoons sugar
pinch of kosher salt

> Find a meat department that will prep your meat, and then treat them like they are the most amazing people in the whole world.

Directions

1. Combine soy sauce, water, honey, brown sugar, sriracha, garlic, and ginger in a small bowl. In a gallon-sized resealable bag, add steak and cornstarch and shake to coat the steak. Add oil to the pressure cooker pot and select brown. When hot, add steak and brown for 3-4 minutes. Pour in sauce and stir, making sure to scrape up the browned bits on the bottom of the pot. Secure the lid and turn pressure release knob to a sealed position. Cook at high pressure for 10 minutes.

2. When cooking is complete, use a natural release.

3. While meat is resting, cook rice noodles on stove top per package directions.

4. Combine cucumbers, red bell peppers, and carrots in a small bowl. Pour vinegar in bowl and sprinkle vegetables with sugar and salt, stir, and set aside. (This can be done up to 3 days in advance and is actually more flavorful if done at least the day before.)

5. When natural release is complete, remove lid and check consistency of sauce. If sauce is too thin, simmer to thicken. (Can also mix 1 tablespoon of cornstarch with 1 tablespoon water, bring mixture to a simmer using the sauté function, then pour in cornstarch slurry and stir until thick.)

6. To serve, place a serving of noodles on a plate, top with steak and extra sauce, and add a scoop of pickled vegetables on the side. Add drops of sriracha for more heat.

Pepperoncini Beef Sandwich with Chopped Giardiniera

While I'm still bitter towards this meat for making my pressure cooker seal smell like pepperoncini and beef, I will forever swoon whenever I eat it. The combination of pepperoncini beef with pickled giardiniera, melty provolone cheese, and chipotle mayo makes me feel spoiled every time I enjoy it. So I bought me a spare silicone ring, put the potent smelling seal in a baggie, and designated its purpose in life to making me this sandwich (as well as other odiferous food). Hopefully, I haven't convinced you to avoid this dish, because it's too wonderful not to have at least once a week. Just don't use the same ring to make your family's oatmeal the next morning . . . they'll talk about it bitterly for weeks. This works with a chuck or rump roast. Both become tender and shred very well. A chuck is fattier and more flavorful, but I personally prefer the less greasy results of a rump roast.

Prep: 10 minutes
Pressure: 90 minutes
Total: About 2 hours

Pressure Level: High
Release: Natural
Serves: 6-8

Ingredients

16-ounce jar pepperoncini slices
14½-ounce can beef broth
1 tablespoon dried oregano
½ tablespoon dried parsley
½ tablespoon garlic powder
½ tablespoon onion powder
1 teaspoon dried basil
1 teaspoon lemon pepper seasoning
¼ teaspoon thyme
½ teaspoon pepper

2 teaspoons kosher salt
3-4-pound chuck or rump roast, visible fat removed, cut into 2 pieces
hoagie rolls
chipotle mayonnaise (I like Sir Kensington's chipotle mayonnaise)
16-ounce jar Italian mix giardiniera, drained and chopped
provolone cheese slices

Directions

1. Add entire contents of pepperoncini jar, beef broth, oregano, parsley, garlic powder, onion powder, basil, lemon pepper, thyme, pepper, and salt to the pressure cooker pot. Stir ingredients and add roast pieces. Secure the lid and turn pressure release knob to a sealed position. Cook at high pressure for 90 minutes.

2. When cooking is complete, use a natural release.

3. Place meat on a plate. Use two forks to shred it, then quickly return it to the pot.

4. Preheat broiler. Split buns in half and place under broiler to brown, about 1 minute. Top buns with chipotle mayo, shredded meat, chopped giardiniera, and provolone cheese slices; place under the broiler again to melt the cheese. Serve.

Tips
- When cooking meat, allow pressure to release naturally. This may take 20-30 minutes but it helps ensure juicy, tender meat.
- If meat doesn't shred or isn't as tender as you'd like, return to high pressure for another 10-15 minutes.
- Buy two silicone rings. You can use one for foods likes this with strong smells and save the other for sweet- or mild-smelling foods.

Pizza-Stuffed Frittata

This recipe is for the mamas standing in front of a near empty fridge at dinner time, for the gluten-free individuals who crave all the flavors of pizza, and for those with minimal skills in the kitchen and aren't about to bust out a homemade pizza dough. It's a frittata, which sounds fancy, looks impressive, takes seconds to whip up, and it tastes like pizza. Pressure cookers do amazing things with eggs, and this frittata proves that. So whatever your favorite version of pizza is, take those toppings, mix them into the egg batter, and serve with a big bowl of your favorite pizza sauce. Dinner is served!

Prep: 10 minutes
Pressure: 30 minutes
Total: 50 minutes

Pressure Level: High
Release: 5-minute natural
Serves: 4

Ingredients

9 eggs
1½ cups ricotta
2 cups chopped spinach
1–2 cups extras: pepperoni, ham, pineapple, tomatoes, diced peppers, pickled jalapeños, sausage, etc. (plus extra for topping)
½ teaspoon basil
½ teaspoon oregano

½ teaspoon garlic powder
½ teaspoon salt
¼ teaspoon pepper
¼ cup of mozzarella or cheddar cheese (or a combination of both)
¼ cup freshly grated Parmesan
pizza sauce, for serving

Directions

1. Lightly grease a 7-inch springform pan with nonstick cooking spray.

2. Add eggs and ricotta to a medium bowl and whisk until smooth. Add spinach, desired extras (remember to save some for topping the frittata in step 4), basil, oregano, garlic powder, salt, and pepper; stir to incorporate. Pour into the prepared pan.

3. Add 1 cup of water to the pressure cooker pot and place a trivet inside. Carefully set the springform pan on the trivet. Secure the lid and turn pressure release knob to a sealed position. Cook at high pressure for 30 minutes.

4. When cooking is complete, use a natural release for 5 minutes and then release any remaining pressure. Remove pan from the pressure cooker. Top with reserved extras and mozzarella (or cheddar or mix of both) and Parmesan. Place under the oven broiler to brown the cheese.

5. Serve hot with a side of pizza sauce for drizzling or dipping.

Pork Burrito Bowls

I don't think I have ever ordered a burrito at a restaurant. It's just too much! Oversized and way more food than anyone can ever finish, squished together in one compartment. How can anything shine when mashed together like that? What a tragedy! But a burrito bowl . . . now we're talking! This meat is perfectly seasoned and amazingly versatile and makes the best burrito bowl—ever. I even managed to convince my husband of the ridiculousness of the massive burrito after he experienced this burrito bowl. Although it's entirely possible that he was just agreeing with me to make this thrilling topic of conversation go away as soon as possible.

Prep: 10 minutes
Pressure: 75 minutes
Total: About 2 hours

Pressure Level: High
Release: Natural
Serves: 6-8

Ingredients

3-4 pounds boneless pork loin roast or pork shoulder
1 yellow onion, coarsely chopped
zest and juice of 1 large orange
zest and juice of 2 limes
½ cup chicken broth
5 cloves garlic, whole
1 tablespoon ground cumin
1 tablespoon dried oregano
2 teaspoons salt
2 teaspoons pepper
2 bay leaves

Serve with

Cilantro Lime Rice (page 105)
Refried Beans (page 115)
Garnish: pico de gallo, guacamole, shredded cheese, olives, lettuce, ranch dressing or sour cream, iceberg lettuce, fresh cilantro, lime wedges, or other toppings of choice

Directions

1. Cut the pork loin into 3-4 large chunks; set aside. Add all of the other ingredients to the pressure cooker pot and stir. Add the pork pieces; stir again. Secure the lid and turn the pressure release knob to a sealed position. Cook at high pressure for 75 minutes.

2. When cooking is complete, use a natural release.

3. Using large tongs or a large slotted spoon, remove pork to a 9x13-inch pan with raised edges and shred with two forks.

4. Set a strainer inside of a bowl, and strain the remainder of the pressure cooker pot's contents into the bowl. Discard the solids and pour the liquid over the pork.

5. Serve as is, or to make it extra special, season with a little extra kosher salt and freshly ground black pepper. Preheat the oven broiler. Place the pork under the broiler for about 2 minutes until nicely browned and crisped. Watch closely, so it doesn't burn!

6. To serve, add a scoop of Cilantro Lime Rice to a large single serving bowl. Top with pork and Refried Beans and garnish with desired toppings.

> This meat is equally delicious served on tacos, inside a quesadilla, enchilada, or just on a roll.

> Both pork shoulder and pork loin will shred using this recipe. Pork shoulder is fattier, more flavorful, and shreds more easily. Pork loin will be less greasy, shreds nicely, but isn't quite as tender.

Smoked Paprika "Roasted" Chicken

My freezer is loaded with baggies of shredded chicken from testing a whole "roasted" chicken again and again. I had some steep criteria for this one, and I wanted it just right. It needed it to be moist and flavorful, and I wanted to just throw it in the pressure cooker without the initial browning step. So I went heavy on the seasoning, even got that seasoning under the skin, added the essential aromatics, and what do you know, my absolute favorite roasted chicken of all time! The best part? You can enjoy it for dinner one night and then shred it up to use in countless recipes for the rest of the week (or like I did, portion it into resealable bags and freeze for another time). My kids, who think chicken is good only in nugget form, LOVED this. It always feels good to make the most wearisome critics happy.

Prep: 15 minutes
Pressure: 6-7 minutes per pound
Total: Less than 1 hour
(time varies depending on size of chicken)

Pressure Level: High
Release: Natural
Serves: About 6

Ingredients

1 tablespoon smoked paprika
2 teaspoons kosher salt
½ teaspoon black pepper
½ teaspoon onion powder
½ teaspoon dried thyme
¼ teaspoon garlic powder
¼ teaspoon cayenne powder
4-6-pound whole chicken, giblets discarded
1 onion, halved
3 carrots, cut into 3 pieces each
3 celery stalks, cut into 3 pieces each
1 cup chicken broth

> Shred leftover chicken into bite-sized pieces and use for meals throughout the week, or freeze in 1-2 cup portions for another time.

Directions

1. In a small bowl, combine paprika, salt, pepper, onion powder, thyme, garlic powder, and cayenne; set aside. Pat chicken dry and then rub the seasoning mix all over the chicken, including inside the cavity and under the skin of the chicken breasts.

2. Add onion, carrots, celery, and chicken broth to the pressure cooker pot and place short trivet inside. Place chicken, breast side up, on the trivet. Secure the lid and turn pressure release knob to a sealed position. Cook at high pressure for 6-7 minutes per pound (example: for a 5-pound chicken, cook about 33 minutes).

3. When cooking is complete, use a natural release.

4. Transfer chicken to a carving board. (Chicken can also be placed under the oven broiler and browned to crisp the skin, if desired.) Carve and serve hot.

> Strain the leftover juices and use a large spoon to skim excess fat from the surface of the broth. Save and use as chicken broth for the Creamy Chicken Noodle Soup on page 137!

Sun-dried Tomato and Feta Turkey Burger

My favorite summertime food is a burger. It never gets old, even when it's the same old beef burger with extra mustard and pickled jalapeños. This, coming from the girl who just can't make herself repeat even the most amazing recipes. But when I'm feeling fancy, I turn to a juicy turkey burger stuffed with bits of sun-dried tomato, feta, and spinach. It is the most flavorful burger I have ever had, and it actually makes my very small "make again and again" list. So . . . a burger in the pressure cooker? When I presented my idea, Cami's first word was "hmmm"; second word "gross". Oh, but it's not. This method doesn't save on time when compared to how I used to make it in a skillet. What it does save are grease splatters, smelly hair, and the risk of a dry burger. If my husband's grilling, I'll still send this burger outside, but otherwise, my pressure cooker makes a mean feta-stuffed turkey burger!

Prep: 15 minutes
Pressure: 5 minutes
Total: 25 minutes

Pressure Level: High
Release: Natural
Serves: 4

Ingredients

1 pound lean ground turkey
½ cup crumbled feta cheese
¼ cup sun-dried tomatoes, jarred in oil, drained and chopped
½ cup fresh spinach, chopped
kosher salt
freshly cracked black pepper
whole wheat hamburger buns
whole spinach leaves
1 avocado, mashed

For Sun-dried Tomato Dressing

¼ cup mayo
¼ cup sour cream or plain yogurt
¼ cup sun-dried tomatoes, jarred in oil, drained and chopped
optional: pinch of grill seasoning (any brand will do)

Directions

1. To make Sun-dried Tomato Dressing: Mix all ingredients in a small bowl; set aside. (Can store leftovers in refrigerator for 1 week.)

2. To a medium-sized bowl, add ground turkey, feta, sun-dried tomatoes, chopped spinach, and salt and pepper to taste; mix just until combined. Form into four patties. Season the outsides with extra salt and pepper.

3. Add 1 cup of water to the pressure cooker pot. This is a suggested method of stacking the patties (feel free to do what works for you): trivet, 8-inch perforated pan, two patties, trivet, two patties (make sure there is space between the patties). Secure the lid and cook at high pressure for 5 minutes.

4. When cooking is complete, use a natural release.

5. Preheat oven broiler. Toast hamburger buns under the broiler. On the top bun, smear Sun-dried Tomato Dressing. On the bottom bun, smear mashed avocado and season with salt and pepper; top with spinach leaves, then burger patty. Complete with the top bun and serve.

Teriyaki Fish Tacos with Mango Cucumber Salsa

I'm still on the path of learning to love seafood. I REALLY want to love it. It's so healthy and pretty and flaky and versatile . . . so I battle on, trying new recipes whenever I feel brave or intrigued. I desperately wanted a good fish recipe for this book, so I turned to a fellow pressure cooker genius and friend, Rich Lum. With his year-round access to fresh and affordable fish, he is absolutely THE pro when it comes to cooking it right and making it taste magical. If anyone was gonna be able to write me a recipe to help me fall in love with fish, I knew it would be him. And I'll be darned, this fish taco recipe is brilliant. Flaky fish atop a warmed tortilla, drizzled with sweet and salty teriyaki sauce, and finished off with a fresh, crisp mango cucumber salsa. I've officially joined the fish lover crowd. Thanks, Rich!

Prep: 10 minutes
Pressure: 8 minutes
Total: 25 minutes

Pressure Level: High
Release: Quick
Serves: 2-4

Ingredients

½ cup soy sauce
¼ cup water
¼ cup mirin (can substitute sake or sherry)
1 tablespoon sesame oil
2 teaspoons sesame seeds
1 clove garlic, minced
1 tablespoon freshly grated ginger

2 tablespoons brown sugar
2-3 green onions, minced (reserve some for garnish)
2 salmon or cod fillets (about 8 ounces each)
1 tablespoon corn starch
1 tablespoon water
small flour tortillas
Mango Cucumber Salsa (see recipe below)

Directions

1. In a small bowl, add soy sauce, water, mirin, sesame oil, sesame seeds, garlic, ginger, brown sugar, and green onions; whisk to combine.

2. Place fish in two 6-inch square pans (or two 8-inch mini loaf pans) and pour half of the marinade over the fish (reserve half of the marinade for serving). Allow fish to marinate for 30 minutes in the fridge.

3. Add 1 cup of water to the pressure cooker pot and place trivet inside. Place the prepared pans inside, stacking them to form an X shape. Secure the lid and turn pressure release knob to a sealed position. Cook at high pressure for 8 minutes.

4. While the fish is cooking, pour reserved marinade into a small sauté pan over medium-high heat on the stove top. In a small bowl or measuring cup, mix 1 tablespoon of cornstarch with 1 tablespoon of water and whisk to combine. Once the marinade comes to a simmer, slowly pour in the cornstarch slurry and whisk constantly until thickened, 1–2 minutes. Set aside.

5. When pressure cooking is complete, use a quick release.

6. Place fish on a plate and flake with a fork. Warm the tortillas and then top with fish, a drizzle of thickened teriyaki sauce, and a scoop of Mango Cucumber Salsa. Serve immediately.

Mango Cucumber Salsa

2 ripe mangos, peeled and diced
½ English cucumber, peeled, seeded, and diced
¼ cup red onion, diced
1 jalapeño, seeded and diced
⅛ cup chopped cilantro
juice of ½ lime
salt and pepper to taste

Directions

1. Mix all of the ingredients together and store in the fridge for up to 5 days.

PASTA, GRAINS, AND BEANS

Almond Butter Cherry Bread Pudding

I love to cook and create meals, but I find lunch time to be a total bore and hassle. While I'm satisfied to have a quick and easy smoothie in the middle of the day, my kids don't find that as acceptable, especially if it's green—heaven forbid! So I decided to jazz up the typical peanut butter and jelly sandwich with a super healthy, whole grain bread pudding version. It's simple, quick to throw together, and can even be made in advance to make it a completely fuss-free meal. I've created two versions, which my kids have named the "grown-up version" and the "kids' version."

Prep: 10 minutes
Pressure: 25 minutes
Total: 40 minutes

Pressure Level: High
Release: Quick
Serves: 4–5

Ingredients

3 eggs
½ cup milk
1 tablespoon vanilla extract
½ teaspoon salt
¼ cup almond butter (I use a fresh-ground, unsweetened, unsalted version)
4 cups of bite-sized cubed whole grain bread
2 cups pitted cherries, cut in half
¼ cup sliced or slivered almonds

For Almond Glaze

½ cup powdered sugar
¼ teaspoon almond extract
1–2 tablespoons milk (enough to make it drizzle)

Directions

1. Lightly grease a 7-inch springform pan with nonstick cooking spray. In a separate bowl, whisk eggs, milk, vanilla, salt, and almond butter together, until well combined. Stir in bread cubes, cherries, and almonds. Pour mixture into greased springform pan.

2. Add 1 cup of water to the pressure cooker pot and place a trivet inside. Place prepared springform pan on the trivet. Secure the lid and turn pressure release knob to a sealed position. Cook at high pressure for 25 minutes.

3. Meanwhile, in a bowl or measuring cup, mix together all ingredients for the Almond Glaze.

4. When cooking is complete, use a quick release.

5. Remove the springform ring and serve warm, with a light drizzle of the Almond Glaze. (Optional: Broil the bread pudding for a couple of minutes in the oven to get the yummy, crunchy bites on top!)

"The Kids" Lunch Time Peanut Butter Banana Bread Pudding

In this version, substitute chunky peanut butter and 2 sliced bananas for the almond butter and cherries. Omit almonds and substitute a drizzle of honey or jam for the almond glaze. Yummy!

Cilantro Lime Rice

A pressure cooker does something to brown rice that just isn't achievable with any other method. Before making it this way, I didn't even like brown rice. I found the texture to be seriously lacking and an unsatisfactory substitute for fluffy white rice. Not anymore. Take any favorite white rice classic (like the famous Cilantro Lime Rice), switch it out for brown rice, and get super excited that you actually want to eat whole grain rice from here on out.

Prep: 5 minutes
Pressure: 22 minutes
Total: 35 minutes

Pressure Level: High
Release: Natural
Serves: 6–8

Ingredients

2 cups short grain brown rice (any variety of brown rice will do)
1 can chicken broth
¾ cup water
1 teaspoon salt
4-ounce can chopped chiles
1 cup cilantro, chopped
juice of 1 lime

Directions

1. Add rice, chicken broth, water, salt, and chiles to the pressure cooker pot and stir. Secure the lid and turn pressure release knob to a sealed position. Cook at high pressure for 22 minutes.

2. When cooking is complete, use a natural release.

3. Add cilantro and lime juice; stir. Serve immediately.

This mac and cheese is perfect with any type of roasted vegetable, so feel free to substitute the tomatoes with your own favorite.

The avocado pesto sauce yields much more than will be needed for this recipe, but it freezes beautifully and can be used in so many different ways. I suggest you make the full recipe. This sauce can be made up to a week in advance and stored in a sealed container in the refrigerator.

Mean Green Mac and Cheese

There's an old, tattered blanket that resides in our home. It's faded, its pattern is dated, and it's held together by yarn ties throughout (of which half are missing). But it was my husband's as a child, so we hold on to it and use it mostly for making indoor forts and covering the couch when kids have the stomach flu. This blanket is lovingly called Mean Green, and as a result, my kids call many of the green things in their life "mean." Mean green shoes, mean green bike, mean green smoothie (also called the STOP-RUINING-MY-SMOOTHIE-WITH-SPINACH! smoothie). So naturally the name of my favorite green version of Mac and Cheese that is dressed with a cheesy, creamy, avocado pesto sauce, is called "Mean Green." Top it all off with roasted tomatoes (of any color, size, or shape), and I am one happy mama. And for a moment, I just might gaze upon mean green blankie's bits of string, batting, and fabric scattered about my house fondly . . . but only for a moment, before I return to my plots of how to make the blankie inconspicuously disappear.

Prep: 10 minutes
Pressure: Varies (see below)
Total: 20 minutes

Pressure Level: High
Release: Quick
Serves: 6

Ingredients

1 pound whole grain uncooked pasta (elbow shape or something similar in size)
4 cups chicken broth
1 tablespoon kosher salt
2 tablespoons butter
½ cup milk (skim, 1%, 2%, or nondairy milks also work)
¼ cup whipped cream cheese
1 cup quesadilla cheese (like Cacique® queso quesadilla or Supremo® queso Chihuahua quesadilla cheese, or substitute with Monterey Jack)
½ recipe Avocado Pesto Sauce

For Roasted Tomatoes

tomatoes of choice (Roma, grape, heirloom, etc.), sliced or halved
olive oil
salt and pepper

For Avocado Pesto Sauce

1 avocado, pitted and flesh scooped out
½ cup packed parsley
½ cup packed cilantro
1 jalapeño, ribs and seeds removed (can leave whole, if more spice is desired)
2 cloves garlic
juice of 2 limes
½ cup water
½ cup olive oil
1 teaspoon salt
½ cup nuts (roasted pistachios are my favorite)

Directions

1. Preheat oven to 425°F. Place tomatoes on a baking sheet lined with nonstick foil or sprayed with nonstick cooking spray. Drizzle with olive oil; toss to coat. Season with salt and pepper. Place in oven for 10–15 minutes to warm and concentrate flavors.

2. Add pasta, chicken broth, kosher salt, and butter to the pressure cooker pot and stir. Secure the lid and turn pressure release knob to a sealed position. Cook at high pressure for half of the pasta package cooking time, minus 1 minute. (Example: If cook time is 16 minutes, cook for 7 minutes.)

3. Meanwhile, prepare the Avocado Pesto Sauce by pulsing all ingredients, except the nuts, in a food processor until smooth. Add nuts and pulse until mostly smooth. This can also be done several days in advance.

4. When pressure cooking is complete, use a quick release. If liquid sprays from valve, close valve, wait 30–60 seconds, and try again. If pasta isn't done, use sauté function to finish cooking with the lid off for 2–3 more minutes.

5. Select sauté function and add milk, cream cheese, quesadilla cheese, and Avocado Pesto Sauce; stir until melted and creamy. Add extra milk if needed.

6. Serve immediately, topped with Roasted Tomatoes.

Mexican Rice

In my ideal world, every Mexican dish needs to be accompanied by refried beans and Mexican rice. I can't remember the last time I actually ate at a Mexican restaurant (how could I, with a new Thai restaurant in town!), but at home, Mexican food is one of my absolute favorite meals. This rice makes the perfect pairing—good spice, but not spicy, extra tomato chunks, whole grain Mexican rice. This is ready to complement any Mexican-style dinner.

Prep: 10 minutes
Pressure: 22 minutes
Total: 45 minutes

Release: Natural
Serves: About 6-8

Ingredients

1 tablespoon olive oil
½ cup diced yellow onion
2 cups short grain brown rice (or other brown rice variety)
10-ounce can diced tomatoes and green chiles
   (I typically use RO-TEL® brand)
14-ounce can diced tomatoes
2 cups chicken broth
1 teaspoon chili powder
1 teaspoon cumin
2 teaspoon kosher salt

> This makes a big batch of rice and freezes very well. Put leftovers in a gallon-sized resealable freezer bag, press flat, and label for a quick side to your next Mexican dinner night!

Directions

1. Select sauté on the pressure cooker and add oil. When hot, add onion and sauté until soft, about 3-4 minutes.

2. Add rice, both cans of tomatoes, chicken broth, chili powder, cumin, and salt. Secure the lid and turn pressure release knob to a sealed position. Cook at high pressure for 22 minutes.

3. When cooking is complete, use a natural release.

4. Stir well and season to taste with extra salt and pepper. Serve warm.

Quinoa Fried Rice

My family wouldn't join me on the quinoa train for a long time. I'd tell my husband, "It's got more protein in it than all the meat you ate this week combined" (a lie). To the kids, I would say, "It's like rice, but in cute ball shapes," 'cause what kid wouldn't be thrilled to eat cute ball-shaped rice. My daughter sweetly replied, "That is NOT rice, I don't want any, no thank you." And yes, that is how she said it—she's a table manners angel, when she wants to be. Unfortunately, her little brothers mimic everything she does, so they had no choice but to join the quinoa-hater club. Well, I'm happy to say, they're all finding their way slowly, and for my daughter and her little copycat crew, this recipe was a win. My daughter won't even touch a green pea, but she'll eat an entire package of edamame and would drink soy sauce from the bottle, if I let her. Well, at least until her grandma told her that it would increase her blood pressure; now she's a tiny bit scared of it. Amazingly, this quinoa dish is 5 for 5 in my home, which happens close to never.

Prep: 10 minutes
Pressure: 1 minute
Total: 20 minutes

Pressure Level: High
Release: 5-minute natural
Serves: 6

Ingredients
1 tablespoon sesame oil
2 cloves garlic, minced
1 tablespoon grated ginger
1½ cups quinoa (rinse if it's not pre-rinsed)
15-ounce can chicken broth
1 cup diced carrots
1 cup frozen shelled edamame
4 eggs, whisked, seasoned lightly with salt and pepper
½ tablespoon rice vinegar
3 tablespoons soy sauce
1-2 tablespoons wasabi paste (optional)

> Eggs can also be cooked after the quinoa and vegetables are done. Push quinoa to the side of the pot, select sauté, and add an extra teaspoon of sesame oil. Add the eggs and stir until almost done, then combine with the quinoa.

Directions

1. Select sauté and add sesame oil to the pressure cooker pot. When hot, add garlic and ginger; stir for 1 minute. Turn pressure cooker off; add quinoa, chicken broth, carrots, and edamame; stir. Place a trivet on top.

2. Pour eggs into an 8-inch perforated pan or 7-inch springform pan lined with nonstick tin foil. Place pan on top of the trivet. Secure the lid and turn pressure release knob to a sealed position. Cook at high pressure for 1 minute.

3. When cooking is complete, use a natural release for 5 minutes and then release any remaining pressure.

4. Remove scrambled egg pouch, pan, and trivet. Using the sauté function, stir the quinoa until any excess liquid has evaporated. Break up the eggs and add to the pot.

5. Add rice vinegar, soy sauce, and wasabi paste; stir. Taste; add more soy sauce if desired. Serve warm.

Quinoa Pizza Bowls

I love quinoa! Not only is it a super punch of protein and whole grains (if you want to get technical, it's actually a seed, but let's not get complicated), but it's sooooo versatile and family friendly. This cheesy, saucy version hits all the important pizza notes and allows everyone involved to customize their own "pizza." Which is a lot less stressful than trying to explain to the pizza guy that I want an Everything Pizza, but leave off the meat and peppers on a quarter of it, no pineapple on another quarter, and then what the heck, just put cheese on the other quarter and put those extra toppings on my "Everything Pizza" quarter. Got that, pizza guy?

Prep: 5-10 minutes
Pressure: 20 minutes
Total: 40 minutes

Pressure Level: High
Release: 10-minute natural
Serves: 1

Ingredients

¼ cup uncooked quinoa (rinse if it's not pre-rinsed)
¼ cup pizza sauce
¼ cup chicken broth
¼ teaspoon salt
2 tablespoons pizza toppings (pepperoni, Canadian bacon, olives, peppers, etc.)
cheese, extra pizza sauce, and any additional toppings, for adding after it's cooked

> The pressure cooker can fit up to six ramekins by putting three on the bottom trivet, then placing a second trivet on top of those, followed by three more ramekins.

Directions

1. Lightly grease a 6-ounce ramekin. Combine quinoa, pizza sauce, chicken broth, and 2 tablespoons of desired toppings in the ramekin.

2. Add 1 cup of water to the pressure cooker pot and place trivet inside. Place ramekin on the trivet. Secure the lid and turn pressure release knob to a sealed position. Cook at high pressure for 20 minutes.

3. When cooking is complete, use a natural release for 10 minutes and then release any remaining pressure.

4. Carefully stir the quinoa. Top with an extra dollop of pizza sauce, cheese, and desired toppings; broil in the oven until the cheese is browned and bubbly, about 1-2 minutes.

Refried Beans

Beans are another one of those foods that I considered poisonous as a child but could now, as an adult, eat four times a week—especially refried beans. Especially **these** *refried beans. Since this recipe, I've become a refried bean snob and no longer find the canned version acceptable. Luckily, these beans freeze and thaw right back to fresh-made status in just a few minutes, so they're ALMOST as easy as opening a can. They are amazing on quesadillas, tacos, burritos, or—my favorite—steaming hot with a big bowl of chips. These beans will be the answer for the moments you realize, oops, I didn't make dinner.*

Prep: 2 minutes
Pressure: 40 minutes
Total: 60 minutes

Pressure Level: High
Release: Natural
Serves: 4-6

Ingredients

2 cups dried black or pinto beans (rinsed and picked clean)
1 small onion, chopped
2 cloves garlic (preferably roasted)
4-ounce can chopped green chiles
2 teaspoons salt
1 teaspoon cumin
½ teaspoon chili powder

> Refried beans freeze very well. Measure 1 cup of refried beans for each sandwich-sized resealable bag. Flatten the bags and freeze.

Directions

1. Add beans, onion, garlic, and chiles to the pressure cooker pot and cover with water by 2 inches. Secure the lid and turn pressure release knob to a sealed position. Cook at high pressure for 40 minutes.

2. When cooking is complete, use a natural release.

3. Place a colander inside a large bowl, pour beans into the colander, and reserve the liquid. Add beans, salt, cumin, and chili powder to a high-powered blender and blend until desired consistency is reached, adding the reserved liquid as needed. Refried beans dry out as they sit, so add a bit more liquid to the blender if they are really thick. Store in a sealed container in the refrigerator.

Roasted Sweet Corn Risotto with Basil

If peaches are the star of summer fruit, sweet fresh corn takes the vegetable category. When combined with risotto that doesn't require all the stirring, stirring, stirring, it's a top-requested summertime meal, for me. My kids request ice pops, but for me, pure joy is sweet roasted corn bathed in cheesy, creamy Arborio rice with a sprinkle of fresh basil. Eat as a main dish, or as a side to grilled lemon chicken, and relish in the fact that risotto now requires less effort than peanut butter and jelly sandwiches.

Prep: 15 minutes
Pressure: 5 minutes
Total: 30 minutes

Pressure Level: High
Release: Quick
Serves: Up to 6

Ingredients

2-3 cups of corn kernels (about 3 medium ears of corn) (may use canned or frozen corn)
1 tablespoon extra virgin olive oil, plus a little more for drizzling over corn
2 tablespoons butter
2 large leeks, white and light green parts only, sliced in half then into thin half moons
½ small onion, chopped

2 cloves garlic, minced
1½ cups Arborio rice
4 cups chicken broth, divided
2 teaspoons kosher salt
1 teaspoon pepper
¼ cup chopped basil
½ cup freshly grated Parmesan cheese, plus a little more for serving

Directions

1. Preheat broiler. Line a baking sheet with nonstick foil or lightly grease with nonstick cooking spray. Place corn kernels on the baking sheet, drizzle lightly with extra virgin olive oil, and toss to distribute the oil evenly; season with salt and pepper to taste. Place under broiler until corn starts to brown, about 2-3 minutes. Watch closely!

2. Preheat the pressure cooker by selecting sauté. Add the butter and 1 tablespoon of olive oil. When butter is melted and slightly bubbling, add the leeks, onion, and garlic; sauté 5-7 minutes or until tender. Add rice to the pot and stir for 1-2 minutes, until opaque.

3. Add 3 cups of chicken broth, salt, and pepper; stir. Secure the lid and turn pressure release knob to a sealed position. Cook at high pressure for 5 minutes.

4. When cooking is complete, use a quick release. Select sauté and stir in two-thirds of the roasted corn and an extra ½–1 cup of chicken broth; stir for 2 minutes. Unplug the pressure cooker; stir in the basil and Parmesan cheese.

5. Serve immediately, topped with an extra sprinkle of Parmesan and the reserved roasted corn kernels.

> If you don't want the extra step of roasting the corn, stir it in fresh. It'll still blow your mind!

Spring Green Risotto

The stove top version of this dish was my first experience with risotto and was it ever a good one! It's creamy, bright, and loaded with vegetables. Before my pressure cooker obsession days, I was trying to make it with a pair of two-year-olds on the loose. Trying to stand at the stove top for 30 minutes stirring rice became a seriously anxiety-ridden experience. Zero-impulse-control two-year-old boys can be a scary thing. Scary as in scary mommy, when she sees her new $50 gallon of shampoo dumped in the toilet. All that justifying of why I needed only the best shampoo for my lovely locks, now down the drain, literally. Well, I don't have two-year-olds anymore, but risotto under 30 minutes, with minimal stirring, is still the discovery of the century.

Prep: 15 minutes
Pressure: 5 minutes
Total: 30 minutes

Pressure Level: High
Release: Quick
Serves: Up to 6

Ingredients

2 tablespoons butter
1 tablespoon extra virgin olive oil
½ small onion, chopped
2 large leeks, white and light green parts only, sliced in half then into thin half moons
1½ cups Arborio rice
4 cups chicken broth, divided
zest and juice of 1 medium-sized lemon
2 teaspoons kosher salt

1 teaspoon ground black pepper
1 pound asparagus, cut into 1-inch pieces, tough ends discarded (may substitute with broccoli)
1½ cups frozen peas
⅓ cup whipped cream cheese
½ cup freshly grated Parmesan cheese, plus a little more for serving
1 tablespoon minced fresh chives

Directions

1. Preheat the pressure cooker by selecting sauté. Add the butter and olive oil. When butter is melted and slightly bubbling, add onion and leeks; sauté 5–7 minutes or until tender. Add the rice to the pot and stir for 1–2 minutes until opaque.

2. Add 3 cups of chicken broth, lemon juice, salt, and pepper; stir. Secure the lid and turn pressure release knob to a sealed position. Cook at high pressure for 5 minutes.

3. Meanwhile, place asparagus in a microwave-safe bowl, cover with hot water, and microwave for 3–4 minutes until crisp-tender. Drain and rinse with cold water to stop the cooking.

4. When pressure cooking is complete, use a quick release. Select sauté and add peas, asparagus, and ½–1 cup of chicken broth; stir for 2 minutes. Unplug pressure cooker, add lemon zest, cream cheese, Parmesan cheese, and chives; stir until well incorporated.

5. Serve immediately with an extra sprinkle of Parmesan and a squeeze of lemon.

Sweet Curry Coconut Cashew Rice

You know those recipes that you see and just know, right off the bat, that they're gonna be good? Like so good that you make a point to go to the grocery store and ignore the steaks in your fridge that are expiring at that very moment, but nothing else matters because HELLO! CURRY RICE WITH CASHEWS, COCONUT, AND PINEAPPLE! Those pricey ribeyes can't be dealt with at a time like this. I'm eating rice for dinner tonight! Hopefully the man of the house didn't see that steak was originally on the menu. This rice dish exceeded my expectations with its perfect balance of flavors and its garnish of salty cashews, lime juice, and Dang® Coconut Chips. Seriously people, this recipe is worth disappointing a carnivorous husband.

Prep: 10 minutes
Pressure: 3 minutes
Total: 20 minutes

Pressure Level: High
Release: 10-minute natural
Serves: 4–6

Ingredients

1 cup uncooked long grain white rice
¾ cup lite coconut milk
¾ cup pineapple juice
2 teaspoons Thai red curry paste
½ teaspoon onion powder
1 teaspoon garlic powder
½ teaspoon ground ginger
1 teaspoon salt
¼ teaspoon pepper

Garnish

unsweetened toasted coconut (like Dang® coconut chips)
cilantro, chopped
cashews, salted and roasted
limes, cut into wedges

Directions

1. To the pressure cooker pot, add rice, coconut milk, pineapple juice, curry paste, onion powder, garlic powder, ground ginger, salt, and pepper; stir to combine. Secure the lid and turn pressure release knob to a sealed position. Cook at high pressure for 3 minutes.

2. When cooking is complete, use a natural release for 10 minutes and then release any remaining pressure. Stir well.

3. Garnish individual servings with a sprinkle of coconut flakes, cilantro, cashews, and a squeeze of lime.

> For a complete meal, serve this rice with the Curry Coconut Lime Chicken Tenders from page 71 and a side of grilled pineapple.

Cooking the pasta in milk lends to its creamier texture without the need for cream. However, reduced- or no-fat milk tends to curdle when boiled. Cornstarch helps bind the milk and prevent curdling, which is what makes this recipe work!

Whole Grain Creamy Mac and Cheese with Roasted Panko Parmesan Broccoli

Mac and cheese is one of those foods you can serve and make just about everybody happy. Since my kids request some version of pasta and cheese daily, I set out to create a healthier, whole grain, less rich but still creamy version that would satisfy everyone. So, here's the setup. First, use your favorite whole grain pasta (our favorite is Tinkyada® Brown Rice Pasta). Next, to make this mac and cheese reduced fat, we're gonna cook it in skim milk, add a little cornstarch, and use a quesadilla-style cheese that melts like a dream! (If you can't find this type of cheese, Monterey Jack cheese will work.) Finally, to mimic the effect of the buttery breadcrumb topping I so adore, I added cheesy panko crusted, roasted broccoli! Yes! Go ahead, drop the mic . . . well, large serving spoon . . . and walk away, baby! Or, don't do this if your ego is going to be destroyed by the blank stares and eye rolls aimed your way by those that are supposed to love you most. Love you, kids!

Prep: 10 minutes
Pressure : Varies (see below)
Total: 20 minutes

Pressure Level: High
Release: Quick
Serves: 6

Ingredients
1 pound of uncooked whole wheat macaroni
2 tablespoons butter
1 tablespoon kosher salt
1 teaspoon dry mustard
¼ teaspoon cayenne
½ teaspoon garlic powder
2 tablespoons cornstarch
2½ cups water
3 cups skim milk, divided
2 cups shredded extra sharp cheddar cheese
1 cup shredded quesadilla cheese (like Cacique®
    queso quesadilla cheese or Supremo® queso
    Chihuahua quesadillia cheese, or can substitute
    with Monterey Jack)

For Roasted Panko Parmesan Broccoli
4 cups broccoli florets
olive oil to lightly coat
¼ cup whole wheat panko breadcrumbs
¼ cup finely grated Parmesan cheese
½ teaspoon dry Italian seasoning
kosher salt
freshly ground black pepper

Directions

1. Preheat oven to 425°F. Line a baking sheet with nonstick foil or spray with nonstick cooking spray.

2. Place broccoli florets in a gallon-sized resealable bag, drizzle with olive oil, seal, and shake to coat. Add panko breadcrumbs, Parmesan cheese, and Italian seasoning; reseal and shake to coat. There will be loose crumbs leftover in the bag, which will be sprinkled on top of the finished mac and cheese.

3. Dump broccoli and crumbs onto the prepared baking sheet. Season with kosher salt and freshly ground black pepper. Roast for 10–15 minutes, watching closely so the crumbs don't burn.

4. While broccoli is roasting, add the macaroni, butter, salt, dry mustard, cayenne, garlic powder, cornstarch, 2½ cups of water, and only 2 cups of milk to the pressure cooker pot. Stir well to incorporate cornstarch.

5. Secure the lid and turn pressure release knob to a sealed position. Cook at high pressure for half of the pasta package cooking time minus 1 minute. (Example: If cook time is 16 minutes, cook for 7 minutes. If it says 12–13 minutes, cook for 6 minutes).

6. When cooking is complete, use a quick release. If liquid sprays from valve, close valve, wait 30–60 seconds, and try again. If pasta isn't done, use sauté function to cook with the lid off for 2–3 more minutes.

7. Select sauté function and add ½ cup of milk (adding another ½ cup, if needed), cheddar, and quesadilla cheese; stir until melted and creamy.

8. Serve immediately, topped with the roasted broccoli and extra crumbs.

SOUPS

Creamy Enchilada Soup

While I'm not into hiding my kids' veggies in their food, I'm 100% into pretending I don't understand or hear the question "So what exactly is in this?" until after they've tried their food and decided they like it. Which is how this soup experience went down. Butternut squash, onions, chiles, red bell peppers, garlic, and potatoes get blended into the base until it's so perfectly silky and rich (with absolutely no cream!), and all my kids see are white beans and juicy chunks of chicken. Top it with cheese and crushed chips, and they'll eat three bowls of it! Of course, my bowl tops out at 10 veggies after I add pico de gallo, avocado, corn, sour cream, cheese, hot sauce, and crushed whole grain tortilla chips! Heaven in a bowl right there! And if you've ever debated whether an immersion blender was worth owning, this recipe, that you will likely make again and again, will be the perfect time to take that plunge.

Prep: 15 minutes
Pressure: 20 minutes
Total: 60 minutes

Pressure Level: High
Release: Natural (or 10-minute natural)
Serves: About 8

Ingredients

4 cups low-sodium chicken broth
3 medium-sized boneless, skinless chicken breasts
3½-ounce can chopped green chiles
1 yellow onion, coarsely chopped
3 large russet potatoes, peeled and quartered
1 red bell pepper, cored, seeded, and coarsely chopped
8 cups peeled, cubed butternut squash (about 24 ounces)
3 cloves garlic

2 teaspoons salt
2 teaspoons cumin
8-ounce can tomato sauce
2 tablespoons taco seasoning (store-bought or homemade version to follow)
2 15-ounce cans cannellini beans, rinsed and drained
additional toppings: shredded cheese, fresh or canned corn, pico de gallo, diced avocado, whole grain tortilla chips, sour cream, Cholula® hot sauce, etc.

Directions

1. Add chicken broth, chicken, green chiles, onion, potatoes, bell pepper, squash, garlic, salt, cumin, tomato sauce, and taco seasoning to the pressure cooker pot; lightly stir.

2. Secure the lid and turn pressure release knob to a sealed position. Cook at high pressure for 20 minutes.

3. When cooking is complete, use a natural release. Can also use a natural release for 10 minutes and then release any remaining pressure.

4. Remove chicken and place on a cutting board, cover with foil. Using an immersion blender, blend soup until very smooth. (This can also be done in batches with a blender. Be careful not to overfill the blender! Place a towel over the lid and gently pulse before turning the speed up to blend.) Chop or shred chicken and return it to the pot of soup. Add cannellini beans and stir.

5. To serve, ladle soup into a bowl, instantly sprinkle with cheese, and top with desired toppings.

Recommended order of toppings

Homemade Taco Seasoning

1 tablespoon chili powder
1 teaspoon ground cumin
1 teaspoon garlic powder
1 teaspoon smoked paprika
½ teaspoon oregano

½ teaspoon onion powder
¼ teaspoon salt
¼ teaspoon black pepper
¼ teaspoon crushed red pepper flakes

Directions

1. Whisk all of the ingredients together until combined and store in an airtight container.

Cabbage Roll Soup

My early memories of cabbage kept me from loving it for many years. To this day, I still don't know what my dad was cooking that smelled so horrific, but I knew it involved sauerkraut which I knew was a form of cabbage; therefore, I hated cabbage. My sisters and I would whine dramatically and lock ourselves in our room to hopefully create one room in the house that wasn't permeated by the ghastly smell. Meanwhile, my dad congratulated himself on creating a peaceful environment for himself to enjoy his meal (that I never saw because I was in voluntary confinement). I'm still not a fan of how cabbage smells, but I could eat a giant plate of steamed cabbage with butter and salt. This recipe is simple as can be and highlights cabbage in a most wonderful way. Trust me when I say that 20 minutes isn't going to overcook your cabbage as long as you coarsely chop it and leave it sitting on top of the liquids. The end result is perfectly soft, large pieces of cabbage that soak up this dreamy tomato-based broth. I highly suggest serving it with a loaf of crusty bread and letting that be your spoon. Yum!

Prep: 15 minutes
Pressure: 20 minutes
Total: 45 minutes

Pressure Level: High
Release: 10-minute natural
Serves: 8

Ingredients

1 teaspoon oil
1 cup diced onion
3 cloves garlic, minced
1 pound lean ground pork
2 teaspoons paprika
1 teaspoon thyme
1 tablespoon kosher salt
1 teaspoon pepper
¾ cup wild rice

28-ounce can diced tomatoes
3 tablespoons tomato paste
4 cups beef broth
2 cups V8® juice
1 tablespoon white wine vinegar
2 tablespoons Worcestershire sauce
1 bay leaf
1 medium head cabbage, core removed and coarsely chopped

Directions

1. Select sauté on the pressure cooker and add oil. When hot, add onions, garlic, and pork. Sprinkle paprika, thyme, salt, and pepper on the pork. Brown and crumble the pork until it's cooked through and until onions are soft. Add rice, diced tomatoes, tomato paste, broth, V8®, vinegar, Worcestershire sauce, and bay leaf; stir. Place chopped cabbage on top—don't stir. Secure the lid and turn pressure release knob to a sealed position. Cook at high pressure for 20 minutes.

2. When cooking is complete, use a natural release for 10 minutes and then release any remaining pressure.

3. Remove bay leaf and serve hot. Add salt and pepper to taste.

Cauliflower Gnocchi Soup with White Cheddar Crisps

A top request by my sister Cami was cauliflower soup. Since I have this nagging desire to take things too far, I invented a roasted cauliflower soup with gnocchi and white cheddar crisps. I don't typically order soup at a restaurant, but if I saw that kind of title on a menu, I'd order two bowls! This creamy cauliflower soup is made with absolutely no cream, just a whole lot of vegetables. It's good enough to eat in the dead of winter or on the back porch in 100-degree heat. Temperature wouldn't even matter because, hello, Cheddar Crisps!

Prep: 15 minutes
Pressure: 10 minutes
Total: 30 minutes

Pressure Level: High
Release: 10-minute natural
Serves: 6

Ingredients
2 tablespoons extra virgin olive oil
1 sweet or yellow onion, diced
2-3 small leeks, white and light green parts only, cut into
   half-moon shapes
2 cloves garlic, minced
kosher salt and freshly ground black pepper
1 medium-sized head of cauliflower, cut into florets
6 cups chicken broth
1 teaspoon dried dill
8-ounce package mini potato gnocchi (not frozen)
lemon slices

> For an extra depth of flavor, toss cauliflower in olive oil to coat. Place on sheet pan, season with salt and pepper, and roast under the broiler until nicely browned. Add to the pot with the broth and dill and proceed with original directions.

Directions

1. Preheat the pressure cooker by selecting sauté. Add oil. When hot, add onion and leeks; sauté until softened, 8–10 minutes. Add garlic and stir for 1 minute. Season with salt and pepper.

2. Add cauliflower, chicken broth, and dill. Secure the lid and turn pressure release knob to a sealed position. Cook at high pressure for 10 minutes.

3. When cooking is complete, use a natural release for 10 minutes and then release any remaining pressure.

4. Carefully pour or ladle pot contents into a blender (be sure not to overfill blender; do in batches if needed). Place a hand towel over the lid to prevent any splatters. Process until very smooth, about 2 minutes. (This can also be done directly in the pot with an immersion blender.) Pour soup back into the pressure cooker pot.

5. Bring soup to a boil by selecting either sauté or brown. Add gnocchi and simmer 2 minutes or until gnocchi float to the top. Taste and adjust seasoning as desired.

6. Serve hot with a squeeze of lemon and top with Cheese Crisps.

White Cheddar Crisps
about 1 cup shredded sharp white cheddar cheese

Directions

1. Preheat oven to 350°F. Line baking sheet with parchment paper. Sprinkle about 1 tablespoon of cheese in a mound for each crisp, leaving 1–2 inches between each mound to allow the cheese to spread as it melts. Bake for 5–10 minutes until dark (but not burnt). Blot crisps with paper towel. Allow to cool for ultimate crunchiness.

Cheesy Butternut Squash Ravioli Soup

*Squash and seafood are two foods I try very hard to enjoy. Imagine how shocked I was when this squash soup stole my heart. It's the kind of soup you eat **slooowwwly** because each mouthful is meant to be savored. It's the top requested soup from my husband and kids and the only reason I will be planting butternut squash when I have kids old enough to know not to pull up my hardworking plants.*

Prep: 10 minutes
Pressure: 15 minutes
Total: 30 minutes

Pressure Level: High
Release: Quick
Serves: 6-8

Ingredients

2 teaspoons olive oil
1 cup chopped onion
3 cloves garlic
1 teaspoon dried rosemary, crushed in palm
1 teaspoon dried thyme
½ teaspoon dried sage
1 teaspoon salt

½ teaspoon pepper
24-ounce package cubed butternut squash (or peel and cube a fresh one)
4 cups chicken broth
4 ounces whipped cream cheese
⅓ cup freshly grated Parmesan cheese
16 ounces cheese stuffed ravioli or tortellini

Directions

1. Select sauté on the pressure cooker and add oil. When hot, add onions and garlic and sauté until soft, about 4 minutes.

2. Add rosemary, thyme, sage, salt, pepper, butternut squash, and chicken broth; stir. Secure the lid and turn pressure release knob to a sealed position. Cook at high pressure for 15 minutes.

3. When cooking is complete, use a quick release.

4. Add cream cheese and Parmesan. Blend with an immersion blender right in the pot until very smooth, or carefully pour into a blender and purée until smooth.

5. Press sauté or brown to bring soup to a boil. Add pasta and cook per package instructions.

6. Season to taste and add extra chicken broth to thin, if desired. Serve hot with extra, extra, extra fresh cracked black pepper.

Creamy Broccoli Cheddar Soup

This is one of several soup recipes in this book whose creaminess delights me to the core, thanks to the vegetable itself. Buttery croutons were all my kids needed to be totally on board with this soup. I still have a perfect image in my memory of green soup all over their cute little faces, hands, and shirts while they ate. Because of course, there's no time for napkins, when buttery croutons dipped in velvety broccoli soup are at stake. Can't say I disagree with them; in fact, I now regret not joining in on the mess. It probably does taste even better when it's in your hair.

Prep: 10 minutes
Pressure: 10 minutes
Total: 30 minutes

Pressure Level: High
Release: 10-minute natural
Serves: 4-6

Ingredients

2 tablespoons butter
1 head broccoli (1½–2 pounds), stems sliced into ½-inch discs, florets separated
½ sweet or yellow onion, diced
2 teaspoons dry mustard
¼ teaspoon cayenne

kosher salt and freshly ground black pepper
2 cups chicken stock
2 cups fresh spinach
1 cup grated sharp cheddar cheese, plus more for topping
croutons (preferably homemade)

Directions

1. Preheat the pressure cooker by selecting sauté. Melt butter and add broccoli stems, onion, dry mustard, cayenne, and large pinch of salt and pepper; sauté for 5 minutes or until onions start to soften.

2. Add broccoli florets and chicken stock. Secure the lid and turn pressure release knob to a sealed position. Cook at high pressure for 10 minutes.

3. When cooking is complete, use a natural release for 10 minutes and then release any remaining pressure.

4. Carefully pour or ladle pot contents into a blender (be sure not to overfill blender; do in batches if needed), or use an immersion blender directly in the pot. Add spinach and cheddar. If using a regular blender, place a hand towel over the lid to prevent any splatters. Process until very smooth, about 2-3 minutes. Add extra chicken broth to thin, if desired. Taste and adjust seasoning as desired.

5. Serve hot with a sprinkle of cheddar cheese and a handful of croutons.

Using the broccoli stalk makes the soup creamy without using any cream.

Creamy Chicken Noodle Soup

Heaven knows why I love to make things like shakshuka, sushi, and homemade butternut squash ravioli, but I still think chicken noodle soup seems so labor intensive. Lucky for me, this is Cami's recipe, and all I have to do to get it is volunteer to whip up some homemade rolls on a Sunday evening, and she'll make a big ol' batch of it. Then for a few hours we can pretend that Cami is the chef and I know something about paint color, mixing textures, and whipping up dreamy curtains (when in reality my young kids' art work is prettier than my attempts at decorating).

Prep: 15 minutes
Pressure: 5 minutes
Total: 40 minutes

Pressure Level: High
Release: 5-minute natural
Serves: 6–8

Ingredients

32 ounces chicken stock
2 cubes chicken bouillon
2 heaping cups chopped carrots
2 cups chopped celery
½ medium onion, finely chopped
1 pound raw chicken tenders

12-ounce package egg noodles
1 tablespoon olive oil
2 cups frozen peas
2 (10-ounce) cans of cream of chicken soup
¾ cup evaporated milk
salt and pepper, to taste

Directions

1. Add chicken stock and bouillon cubes to the pressure cooker pot. Using the sauté or simmer function, simmer until the cubes are dissolved. Add carrots, celery, onion, and chicken tenders; stir. Cook at high pressure for 5 minutes.

2. Fill a large pot with water and add 2–3 large pinches of salt. On a stove top, bring the water to a boil; add pasta and cook according to package directions. When tender, drain the pasta and toss with 1 tablespoon of oil to prevent the pasta from sticking. Set aside.

3. When pressure cooking is complete, use a natural release for 5 minutes and then release any remaining pressure. If liquid sprays from the valve, turn knob back to a sealed position and wait another 5 minutes before opening again.

4. Remove chicken from pot and cut or shred into bite-sized pieces. Return chicken to pot.

5. Stir in peas, cream of chicken soup, evaporated milk, and salt and pepper to taste. Using the sauté or simmer function, simmer until the soup reaches desired temperature.

6. To serve, ladle soup into bowls and add desired amount of noodles.

> Store leftovers in the fridge for up to 5 days, or in the freezer for 2 months or so. Keep noodles separated from the soup during storage.

Creamy Zucchini Spinach Soup

Green is now the new red when it comes to dipping my grilled cheese sandwiches. Translation: I'm confidently predicting that grilled cheese dipped in zucchini spinach soup is about to trample the historical tradition of tomato soup. I still adore tomato soup, but man oh man is this soup a complete treat! I was suspicious at first, as you might be, but be brave. You're likely gonna have a plethora of zucchini at some point, either from your garden or your neighbor's, and this is a perfect place to use it.

Prep: 10 minutes
Pressure: 5 minutes
Total: 30 minutes

Pressure Level: High
Release: 10-minute natural
Serves: About 6

Ingredients

2 tablespoons olive oil
3 medium leeks, white and light green parts only, sliced in half then into thin half moons
2 cloves garlic (preferably roasted)
4 medium zucchini, ends trimmed and coarsely chopped (about 6-7 cups)
2 teaspoons salt
1 teaspoon pepper
4 cups chicken broth
¼ cup fresh basil
3-4 cups fresh spinach, coarsely chopped, divided
optional toppings: sour cream, ricotta

> This soup is an amazing base for all kinds of extras. Think cheese-stuffed pasta, penne, roasted vegetables, shredded rotisserie chicken, etc.

Directions

1. Select sauté on the pressure cooker and add oil. When hot, add leeks and garlic and sauté until softened, about 3-4 minutes. Add zucchini, salt, pepper, and chicken broth. Secure the lid and turn pressure release knob to a sealed position. Cook at high pressure for 5 minutes.

2. When cooking is complete, use a natural release for 10 minutes and then release any remaining pressure.

3. Add basil and 1 cup of the spinach. Blend with an immersion blender right in the pot until very smooth. Alternatively, carefully pour into a blender and purée until smooth. Stir in remaining spinach and add extra broth if a thinner consistency is desired.

4. Serve hot with a drizzle of sour cream or a scoop of ricotta.

Rainbow Thai Soup

When my husband and I go on our motorcycle adventures, we make a point to hit a new Thai restaurant, every night if possible. It rarely disappoints, and it's led to a more adventurous side of me in the kitchen. I hardly knew what curry, fish sauce, and oyster sauce were two years ago, and now they're part of my kitchen essentials. This colorful soup is loaded with vegetables of every color and has the most perfect amount of spicy punch. A huge squeeze of lime juice and a handful of roasted peanuts make it the greatest Thai meal, in the comfort of my own home.

Prep: 15 minutes
Pressure: 3 minutes
Total: 30 minutes

Pressure Level: High
Release: 5-10-minute natural
Serves: 6-8

Ingredients

1 can lite coconut milk
4 cups chicken broth
3 large carrots, sliced
1 pound chicken breast, cubed
juice of 2 limes
3 tablespoons soy sauce
1 tablespoon Thai green curry paste
½ teaspoon yellow curry powder
½ teaspoon salt
½ teaspoon pepper
½ teaspoon garlic powder

6 ounces whole wheat spaghetti pasta (or any pasta with box direction cook time of 6-7 minutes), broken in half
1 green bell pepper, sliced into long strips
1 red bell pepper, sliced into long strips
1 yellow bell pepper, sliced into long strips
1 bunch cilantro, chopped
4 green onions, chopped
for serving: lime wedges, soy sauce roasted peanuts, sriracha

Directions

1. Add coconut milk, chicken broth, carrots, chicken, lime juice, soy sauce, curry paste, curry powder, salt, pepper, garlic powder, and pasta to pressure cooker pot; stir. Add sliced bell peppers on top, but do not stir. Secure the lid and turn pressure release knob to a sealed position. Cook at high pressure for 3 minutes.

2. When cooking is complete, use a quick release. If liquid sprays from valve, turn valve back to a sealed position and wait another 5 minutes before opening again.

3. Unplug the pressure cooker and stir in cilantro and green onions. Add extra broth or coconut milk if a thinner soup is desired.

4. Serve in a bowl with an extra squeeze of lime juice and/or generous sprinkle of soy sauce, roasted peanuts, and a few dots of sriracha.

DESSERT

Apple Papplz

My favorite thing about the process of making this cookbook was seeing my kids really get into it. They were my biggest fans and my favorite critics. My young boys showed their support when I fed them something they loved by saying, "Mom! You've gotta put this one in your cookbook." However, several times they said that about drive-through hamburgers, store-bought cereal, grilled cheese sandwiches, and ice cream. Oh, how I love the sweet innocence of a young child's mind! My daughter, however, knew exactly what was going on. One night she set out to make the perfect pressure cooker creation. She chopped, mixed, and scooped everything all by herself and BEAMED with pride at what she had created. And I will agree that it was straight-up delicious, and it's with tears in my eyes and a very full heart, that I present to you her Apple Papplz.

In the words of my daughter: "I love Apple Papplz. They have sweet tastings with peanut butter and chocolate. Enjoy!"

Prep: 5 minutes
Pressure: 2 minutes
Total: 10 minutes

Pressure Level: High
Release: Quick
Serves: 6

Ingredients

3 large apples, coarsely chopped
24 Ghirardelli® white chocolate melting wafers
6 tablespoons unsweetened peanut butter

> Tip (from my daughter): "You can add whatever toppings you want! Sprinkles, strawberries, whipped cream, toffee bits. . . . It tastes like heaven!"

Directions

1. Spray six 6-ounce ramekins with cooking spray. Set aside.

2. Divide apples between ramekins and top each with 4 white chocolate wafers and 1 tablespoon of peanut butter.

3. Add 1 cup of water to the pressure cooker pot and place a trivet inside. Place three ramekins on the trivet, top with another trivet, follow with three more ramekins. Secure the lid and turn pressure release knob to a sealed position. Cook at high pressure for 2 minutes.

4. When cooking is complete, use a quick release.

5. Carefully remove ramekins and serve hot with a scoop of ice cream.

Chocolate Fudge Lava Cake

Most people around me know that I live a low to no added sugar lifestyle, so this one is for the kids. "What recipe do you want me to make for the book?" Silly son says: "The volcano river one." Logical son: "It's not called a volcano river." Silly son: "Okay, the chocolate volcano one." Logical son: "That's not right either." Silly son: "Then what's it called?" Logical son: "I'm not telling you" (because he doesn't have a clue). Know-it-all daughter: "Volcanos don't have chocolate, they have fire water." Silence . . . "So you guys want lava cake?" "YES!" This was the first time I'd made it in a pressure cooker instead of an oven, and it was also the first time I successfully got it out of its cooking vessel without breaking it prematurely. The pressure cooker produces a moist fudgy exterior with a silky river of chocolate inside. It's my new favorite way to make these cakes and my go-to from now on.

Prep: 15 minutes
Pressure: 5-6 minutes
Total: 25 minutes

Pressure Level: High
Release: Quick
Serves: 6

Ingredients

6 ounces good quality bittersweet chocolate, chopped (I've used up to 85% and 90% chocolate with great results)
8 tablespoons butter
large pinch of kosher salt
1 teaspoon vanilla extract
3 eggs

3 egg yolks
1½ cups powdered sugar
½ cup all-purpose flour
optional toppings: ice cream, whipped cream, powdered sugar, berries, caramel, hot fudge, cookie crumbs, sprinkles, etc.

Directions

1. Grease bottom and sides of six 6-ounce ramekins with nonstick cooking spray and set aside.

2. In a small saucepan over medium heat, melt the chocolate and butter together, stirring constantly until smooth. Take off the heat and stir in salt and vanilla. Set aside.

3. In a blender, add eggs and egg yolks. Blend at medium speed for 1-2 minutes until thick and light in color. Add the powdered sugar and pulse to combine. Add the cooled, melted chocolate and blend for 30 seconds until smooth and incorporated. Add flour and pulse, only until combined. This process could also be done with a bowl and a hand mixer.

4. Fill each ramekin about two thirds full.

5. Add 1 cup of water to the pressure cooker pot and place trivet inside. Place three ramekins on top of the trivet followed by a second trivet and three more ramekins. Secure the lid and turn the pressure release knob to a sealed position. Cook at high pressure for 5-6 minutes.

6. When cooking is complete, use a quick release.

7. Check cakes. The sides should be set and the center slightly soft. If batter still appears runny, cook for 1 more minute. If cake is overcooked, it will still be fudgy and delicious, but it won't have the molten filling.

8. Invert a plate on top of the ramekin and gently flip it over to allow the cake to fall onto the plate. Serve hot with a scoop of ice cream and desired toppings.

Coconut Vanilla Rice Pudding

When Cami suggested we make this cookbook, I was all about it. But more in a "Yeah, for sure we should do that or just think about it or talk about how cool it would be" kind of way. This wouldn't have happened without her and the hundreds of hours she has poured into it, so of course I had to ask, "Cami, what recipe can I create for you?" The answer came immediately— "Rice pudding"—and my mind instantly started thinking about how I could use brown rice, sweeten it with pureed fruit, add some chia seeds . . . "But not a healthy one," she interrupted, "Just a really good rice pudding, like it's meant to be." What! But why? Well, okay. So with a little bit of healthy and a whole lot of delicious, this one's for you Cami. Thanks for inspiring me to go after my dreams. I couldn't have done this without you.

Prep: 10 minutes
Pressure: 10 minutes
Total: 30 minutes

Pressure Level: High
Release: 10-minute natural
Serves: About 6

Ingredients
1 cup Arborio rice
14-ounce can lite coconut milk
1½ cups water
pinch of salt
½ cup honey or agave
1 tablespoon vanilla extract

½–1 cup milk (any kind, but unsweetened vanilla almond cashew milk is creamy and delicious)
chopped mango or chopped strawberries
unsweetened toasted coconut (like Dang® coconut chips)

Directions

1. Add rice, coconut milk, water, salt, honey (or agave), and vanilla to the pressure cooker pot and stir. Secure the lid and turn pressure cooker release knob to a sealed position. Cook at high pressure for 10 minutes.

2. When cooking is complete, use a natural release for 10 minutes and then release any remaining pressure. Select sauté and stir in an extra ½–1 cup of milk to reach desired consistency. Unplug the pressure cooker.

3. Serve warm topped with chopped mangos or strawberries and coconut. Pudding will thicken as it cools.

> This pudding is also wonderful chilled with a drizzle of Coconut Vanilla Syrup (page 13).

German Chocolate Cheesecake

*My man loves his desserts, but only top-notch, homemade, five-star desserts. Don't offend him with ice pops, store-bought pies, packaged cookies, etc. because you're gonna get "the look" that means, "I won't make eye contact with you because I'm so bugged right now." So, when I asked him what he wanted me to make especially for him, he immediately said German chocolate cake. Hmm . . . I don't think I can make that in the pressure cooker. But I **had** been wanting to try out a cheesecake, so the ultimate pressure cooker dessert was born. And it was good, really good . . . like, I took a couple of bites and, after being sugar-free for two years, wondered if I was going back kind of **good**. This cheesecake has all the classic flavors of a German chocolate cake but is rich, fudgy, and completely over the top with that dark ganache spilling over the sides. This cake is gonna win me a ribbon one day, I just know it.*

Prep: 30 minutes
Pressure: 35 minutes
Total: 4 hours (includes chill time)

Pressure Level: High
Release: 10-minute natural
Serves: 6–8

For Crust
1½ cups chocolate wafer cookie crumbs
3 tablespoons butter, melted

For Cheesecake Filling
2 8-ounce packages "⅓ less fat" cream cheese at
    room temperature
⅔ cup sugar
¼ teaspoon salt
1 teaspoon vanilla extract
2 large eggs, room temperature
2 tablespoons cocoa powder
6 ounces German or bittersweet chocolate, melted
    and cooled until just slightly warm

For Coconut Pecan Frosting
2 egg yolks
½ cup sugar
½ cup evaporated milk
¼ cup butter
1 teaspoon vanilla extract
⅔ cup flaked coconut
½ cup chopped pecans

For Chocolate Ganache
¾ cup semisweet chocolate chips
½ cup heavy cream

Directions

1. Spray a 7-inch springform pan with nonstick cooking spray. Line the bottom of the pan with parchment paper for easy removal of the cake once it's done.

2. **To make crust:** Stir cookie crumbs and melted butter together and press evenly across the bottom and halfway up the sides of the pan. Place in the freezer to set (this can be done 2–3 days in advance).

3. **To make cheesecake filling:** Cream the cream cheese with a handheld mixer on low speed until very smooth; scrape the bowl and mix again. Add sugar, salt, and vanilla; continue to scrape and mix the ingredients together on low speed until well combined and smooth. Add eggs, one at a time, continuing to mix and scrape bowl as needed. Mix in cocoa powder until well combined. Finally, add the melted and cooled chocolate and mix just until incorporated. Scrape the bowl and continue to stir by hand until smooth.

4. Remove the pan from the freezer and fill with the cheesecake mixture.

5. Add 1 cup of water to the pressure cooker pot and place trivet inside. Carefully lower the prepared pan onto the trivet. Secure the lid and turn pressure release knob to a sealed position. Cook at high pressure for 35 minutes.

6. **To make Coconut Pecan Frosting:** While cheesecake is cooking, prepare the frosting by combining egg yolks, sugar, evaporated milk, butter, and vanilla in a small saucepan. Cook and stir over medium heat until thickened. This will take 12–15 minutes. Remove from heat, add coconut and pecans, and stir vigorously until well incorporated and silky.

7. When pressure cooking is complete, use a 10-minute natural release and then release any remaining pressure.

8. Remove pan from pressure cooker and let cool for 10 minutes. Slowly remove the springform ring, being careful not to break the crust. Place cheesecake in the refrigerator for at least 4 hours to chill all the way through.

9. When chilled, top with Coconut Pecan Frosting (there's likely to be leftover frosting). Return cheesecake to fridge.

10. **To make chocolate ganache:** Place chocolate chips in a small, heat-safe bowl and set aside. Pour heavy cream into a small saucepan over medium heat and bring to a light simmer. Pour hot cream over the chocolate chips and cover. After 5 minutes, uncover and whisk the chocolate mixture vigorously until smooth and shiny. Let cool and thicken slightly, then drizzle over the Coconut Pecan Frosting on the cake. Can be served immediately or chilled a bit longer to set ganache. This cake is also delicious made one day in advance.

Make Your Own Chocolate Bar

This is another idea that came from my sweet daughter's brain, and I'll admit, the first time she mentioned making a chocolate bar in a pressure cooker, I just smiled and said something lame like, "That sounds fun, what a creative idea!" It took two days for me to realize she just might be onto something. I had a mini bread pan that I placed a few squares of chocolate in, sprinkled it with sliced almonds, and then set it inside the pressure cooker for 2 minutes to see what would happen. Well, it was in fact, genius. It melted into the shape of the pan and once it cooled and hardened, looked like a store-bought chocolate bar. Now, I know there are companies that make a good living off of selling customized chocolate bars, but they are very expensive. Now, I can take my favorite chocolate and mix in my favorite toppings and do it again and again at no extra cost. This is a blast with kids and I have full intentions of doing it for a birthday party one day. In the meantime, I feel like I've gotta come up with a more exciting name for this revolutionary idea that the light of my life daughter came up with. Dream Big Chocolate Bar. Empty the Pantry Chocolate Bar. That Won't Taste Good with Chocolate-Chocolate Bar. Mommy's Break Time Chocolate Bar . . . I guess there's a name for every version!

Prep: 5 minutes
Pressure: 2 minutes
Total: 10 minutes plus chill time

Pressure Level: High
Release: Quick
Makes: Up to 4 chocolate bars at one time

Ingredients

chocolate bar, chocolate chips, or Ghirardelli® chocolate melting wafers (white, dark, milk, mint, butterscotch . . . choose your favorite)

toppings: nuts, sprinkles, coarse sea salt, peanut butter, almond butter, caramel bits, toffee, cacao nibs, marshmallows, cookie crumbs, broken graham crackers, dried bananas, etc.

You will also need mini bread loaf foil or metal pans. (I've also used silicone muffin liners and silicone chocolate molds. Anything small and heat-safe will work.)

Directions

Anything goes for this recipe, I'll just give an idea of how much goes into each bar.

1. Scatter about ½ cup chocolate chips or wafers into the pan or mold (or 3-4 chocolate squares, chopped if thick). Sprinkle on desired toppings.

2. Add 1 cup of water to the pressure cooker pot and place trivet inside. Place two prepared pans inside; top with another trivet followed by two more pans. Optional: cover the chocolate with foil to prevent water dripping into the pans when the lid is removed. Secure the lid and turn pressure release knob to a sealed position. Cook at high pressure for 2 minutes.

3. When cooking is complete, use a quick release.

4. Carefully remove pans and set on a cooling rack. If the chocolate didn't completely melt into a flat layer, use a knife to spread the chocolate smooth. Let the chocolate sit at room temperature until hard, about 1 hour.

5. After hardened, pop out your creations and enjoy!

> After using every type of chocolate in the baking and fancy chocolate bar aisle, I found that Lindt Excellence bars (70%, 85%, and 90%) work the very best. They were the only chocolate that would melt into a luscious chocolate puddle so that when it hardened it looked like a professional chocolate bar. I used about 3-4 squares to make an even row in the pan and then added my toppings. However, my kids like mixing chocolate chip flavors together. After the cooking is done, I use a knife to spread the melted chips into a smooth layer, and for kids, it's perfection.

Favorite Kid Versions

- white chocolate with sprinkles
- dark chocolate with toffee
- milk chocolate with graham crackers and marshmallow (yummy and MESSY)
- zebra (white chocolate and dark chocolate wafers)

My Favorite Versions

- dark chocolate with roasted, salted almonds
- dark chocolate and cacao nibs, sprinkled with coarse sea salt after cooked
- dark chocolate with a couple dollops of almond butter and coarse sea salt
- (noticing a pattern? Dark Chocolate + Salt = Love)

During storage, blooming of the chocolate may occur (separation of sugar or fat content, resulting in inconsistent texture or look). Storing the chocolate in an airtight container at room temperature may help slow and prevent this from happening.

This would be a total hit at a birthday party or for personalized Christmas gifts!

Spiced Poached Pears

Fruit is fabulous all by itself, but magical things happen when it's cooked. Enter: Poached Pears. Warm and juicy with all the comforting flavors of fall, these pears are a home run for dessert, breakfast, lunch, or dinner for that matter. Pears go well with so many different flavors. Topped with a Frozen Whipped Cream Dollop (page 189), ice cream, coconut caramel syrup, frozen blueberries . . . I could go on for days.

Prep: 10 minutes
Pressure: 7 minutes
Total: 20 minutes

Pressure Level: High
Release: Quick
Serves: 4-6

Ingredients

4-6 firm pears
unsweetened apple juice
3 cinnamon sticks
5 whole allspice berries
3 whole cloves
1 vanilla bean, sliced lengthwise
toppings: ice cream, caramel, ground cinnamon

> Play around with new flavors! Add dried cherries or raisins, use cherry or pomegranate juice in place of apple juice, top with cream, toffee bits, and a drizzle of pure maple syrup . . . the possibilities are endless!

Directions

1. Peel pears and leave whole. Cut bottoms, so they sit flat when stem is facing up. Add pears to the pressure cooker pot (stem up) and pour in enough apple juice so three quarters of the pear is covered. Add cinnamon sticks, allspice berries, cloves, and vanilla bean, making sure they are immersed in the apple juice. Secure the lid and turn pressure release knob to a sealed position. Cook at high pressure for 7 minutes.

2. When cooking is complete, use a quick release.

3. Carefully remove the pears from the pot with a slotted spoon. Place a fine mesh strainer over a bowl and pour remaining liquid into the bowl. Reserve liquid for a delicious hot apple cider beverage or for another batch of poached pears. Discard any solid bits left behind in the strainer.

4. Serve pears hot with a scoop of ice cream, drizzle of caramel, and an extra sprinkle of ground cinnamon.

Triple Layer Chocolate Cheesecake

Have you ever noticed how particular people can be about their chocolate? Milk chocolate lovers gag when offered dark; dark chocolate lovers have to buy anything and everything that claims it's dark; white chocolate lovers think they love chocolate, not realizing that white chocolate is hardly chocolate. But everyone can at least agree on the fact that chocolate desserts will never disappoint in a crowd. Like never ever. This cheesecake is a home-run crowd pleaser and will earn you the title of "hero" as you unite all chocolate lovers together in one stunning triple chocolate cake.

Prep: 30 minutes
Pressure: 45 minutes
Total: 70 minutes plus chill time

Pressure Level: High
Release: 10-minute natural
Serves: 12–16

For Crust
4 tablespoons butter, melted
1½ cups chocolate cookie crumbs (I just throw a whole package of Oreos in the food processor, measure out what I need, and freeze the rest.)

For Cheesecake Filling
3 8-ounce packages "⅓ less fat" cream cheese, room temperature
1 cup sugar
2 tablespoons cornstarch
3 large eggs, room temperature
½ cup plain Greek yogurt
1 tablespoon vanilla extract
4 ounces milk chocolate
4 ounces white chocolate
4 ounces bittersweet chocolate (as dark as you can find)

Directions

1. Spray a 7- or 8-inch springform pan with nonstick cooking spray. Line the bottom of the pan with parchment paper for easy removal of the cake once it's done. (See note on next page.)

2. **To make crust:** Stir cookie crumbs and melted butter together and press evenly across the bottom and halfway up the sides of the pan. Place in the freezer to set (this can be done 2–3 days in advance).

3. **To make cheesecake filling:** Cream the cream cheese with a handheld mixer on low speed until very smooth; scrape the bowl and mix again. Add sugar and cornstarch; continue to scrape and mix the ingredients together on low speed until well combined and smooth. Add eggs, one at a time, continuing to mix and scrape bowl as needed. Finally, add yogurt and vanilla and mix just until blended. Scrape the bowl and continue to stir by hand until smooth, if needed.

4. Divide batter into three separate bowls (about 2 cups each). Melt the milk chocolate in the microwave for 30 seconds; stir. Return the chocolate to the microwave for another 15–30 seconds and stir until it is completely melted and smooth. Whisk into one of the bowls of cheesecake batter. Repeat with the white and bittersweet chocolates (each being stirred into a different bowl of batter). Refrigerate the 3 bowls for 15–20 minutes, so they will be more firm for layering.

5. Remove the bowls from the fridge. Take the pan with the crust out of the freezer. Time to layer!

6. Pour dark chocolate batter into the center of the crust and smooth outward to form an even layer. Very carefully spoon dollops of the white chocolate batter on top of the dark chocolate and gently smooth over the top (GENTLY so the layers don't mix together). Repeat with milk chocolate batter.

7. Add 1 cup of water to the pressure cooker pot and place trivet inside. Carefully lower the prepared pan onto the trivet. Secure the lid and turn pressure release knob to a sealed position. Cook at high pressure for 45 minutes.

8. When pressure cooking is complete, use a 10-minute natural release and then release any remaining pressure.

9. Remove pan from pressure cooker and let cool for 10 minutes. Slowly remove the springform ring, being careful not to break the crust. Allow the cake to cool completely and then cover and place in the refrigerator (at least 4 hours; overnight is best).

10. Before serving, let stand at room temperature 30–60 minutes. Top with sugared cranberries, chocolate ribbons, or a chocolate or peanut butter ganache, if desired.

This is a tall cake and will either need to be layered in a 7-inch pan that is greater than 3 inches tall or in an 8-inch pan. Another option is to make thinner layers and then use the leftover to make an extra mini-cheesecake to stash in the freezer for later.

Vanilla Cashew Cream "Cheesecake" with Cherry Compote (no sugar added)

*This "cheesecake" is not for the faint of heart. Some will love it, some will tolerate it, and others—like my hilarious brother—will dump a cup of sugar on it just to make a point. For someone who strives to stick to a naturally sweetened lifestyle, this cake will surely be the love of your life. I adore this cheesecake, and for me, it shines like a diamond in a row of sugar-laden, overindulgent desserts dripping with chocolate and caramel. This cheesecake makes me feel good before, during, and after I've eaten it. In fact, this cheesecake is one I'll eat for dessert with dinner and then let my kids polish off for breakfast the next morning. And don't even get me started on the Cherry Compote! Cherries are one fruit I'll throw in my shopping cart without so much as a glance at the price tag, I love them so much! Fortunately for this compote, frozen cherries are perfect and don't require any laborious pitting. This cheesecake is 100% naturally sweetened and, for me, proves that dessert can be good and good **for** you too.*

Prep: 20 minutes
Pressure: 45 minutes
Total: 70 minutes (plus overnight chill)

Pressure Level: High
Release: 10-minute natural
Serves: 8

For Crust
¾ cup chopped pecans
4 Medjool dates, pitted
2 tablespoons almond flour
2 tablespoons cacao nibs (optional for extra crunch)

For Cashew Cream
1 cup unsweetened vanilla almond milk
15 Medjool dates, pitted
1 cup raw cashews
pinch of kosher salt
1 tablespoon vanilla extract
2 cups Greek yogurt
1 tablespoon tapioca flour

For Cherry Compote
2 cups frozen dark sweet cherries
2 tablespoons water
1 tablespoon maple syrup (optional)

Directions

1. Spray a 7-inch springform pan with nonstick cooking spray. Line the bottom of the pan with parchment paper for easy removal of the cake once it's done.

2. **To make crust:** Add pecans, 4 dates, and almond flour to the bowl of a food processor or blender and pulse until the mixture is crumbly and sticking together. Add cacao nibs, if using, and pulse 3–4 more times to incorporate them into the mixture. Pour the mixture into the springform pan and press evenly across the bottom and halfway up the sides of the pan. Place in the freezer to set (about 30 minutes).

3. **To make cashew cream:** Add almond milk and 15 dates to a high-powered blender and blend until smooth. Scrape the blender and then add cashews, salt, and vanilla. Blend again until very smooth, scraping as needed. Add yogurt and tapioca flour and pulse just to combine.

4. Fill the crust with the cashew cream mixture.

5. Add 1 cup of water to the pressure cooker pot and place trivet inside. Carefully lower the prepared pan onto the trivet. Secure the lid and turn pressure release knob to a sealed position. Cook at high pressure for 45 minutes.

6. When cooking is complete, use a 10-minute natural release and then release any remaining pressure.

7. Remove pan from pressure cooker and let cool for 10 minutes. Slowly remove the springform ring, being careful not to break the crust. Once cooled, cover and place cheesecake in the refrigerator overnight.

8. Top each serving with a scoop of cherry compote.

For the Cherry Compote

This can be made up to 3 days in advance if needed.

1. Add cherries, water, and maple syrup (if using) to the pressure cooker pot and stir. Secure the lid and turn pressure release knob to a sealed position. Cook at high pressure for 2 minutes.

2. When cooking is complete, use a natural release for 5 minutes and then release any remaining pressure.

3. Select sauté and bring compote to a light boil. Simmer for about 1–2 minutes until compote thickens.

The Peach Compote (page 207), Berry Compote (page 4), or the Coconut Vanilla Syrup (page 13) also make an amazing topping!

White Chocolate Vanilla Lava Cake

I'm not new to baking, by any means, but I'd given up on lava cakes. I couldn't ever get the timing right; they always got overbaked and lacked the lava. And if by chance I did get my timing right, I couldn't get them out of the pan without ruining them. Always tasty, just not the showstopper dessert I was going for. The pressure cooker seems to create an ideal environment for the cake to cook moist and soft on the exterior and flowy and rich on the inside. And bonus, they come out of the ramekin like a dream. Showstopper status restored!

Prep: 15 minutes
Pressure: 7–8 minutes
Total: 25 minutes

Pressure Level: High
Release: Quick
Serves: 6

Ingredients

6 ounces white chocolate (good quality), chopped
5 tablespoons butter
1 teaspoon vanilla extract
pinch of kosher salt
2 eggs

2 egg yolks
¼ cup sugar
¼ cup all-purpose flour
optional toppings: vanilla ice cream, lemon zest,
   blueberries

Directions

1. Grease bottom and sides of six 6-ounce ramekins with nonstick cooking spray and set aside.

2. In a small saucepan over medium heat, melt the chocolate and butter together, stirring constantly, until smooth. Take off the heat and stir in vanilla and salt; set aside.

3. In a blender, add eggs and egg yolks. Blend at medium speed for 1–2 minutes, until thick and light in color. Add sugar and blend for another minute. Add the cooled, melted chocolate and blend for 30 seconds until smooth and incorporated. Add flour and pulse, only until combined. This process could also be done with a bowl and a hand mixer.

4. Fill each ramekin about two-thirds full.

5. Add 1 cup of water to the pressure cooker pot and place trivet inside. Place three ramekins on top of the trivet followed by a second trivet and three more ramekins. Secure the lid and turn the pressure release knob to a sealed position. Cook at high pressure for 7–8 minutes.

6. When cooking is complete, use a quick release.

7. Check cakes: the sides should be set and the center slightly soft. If batter still appears runny, cook for 1 more minute. If cake is overcooked, it won't have a molten filling.

8. Invert a plate on top of the ramekin and gently flip it over to allow the cake to fall onto the plate. Serve hot with a scoop of vanilla ice cream, a sprinkle of lemon zest, and blueberries if desired.

> **Tips**
> - The batter can be completely prepared and stored in the refrigerator. If using batter cold, scoop batter into ramekins, flatten slightly, and then cook for 6–7 minutes.
> - Add a piece of caramel or a chocolate square to the center of the cake before cooking for a surprise molten filling.

SAUCES

Barbecue Sauce

I'm a sauce kind of girl. My husband goes with the smallest amount possible on his meat, which I would find completely aggravating, except it ultimately means more sauce for me. In fact, I go as far as giving him half of my meat for half of his sauce, which makes that a quadruple dose of sauce for me . . . Right? Doesn't matter. What does matter is that this barbecue sauce is such a beautiful balance of sweet, spicy, tangy, and smoky. After trying it, you'll completely understand why I use a spoon to eat my barbecue chicken. Because in my world, it's totally normal to eat barbecue sauce like it's a soup.

Prep: 10 minutes
Pressure: 15 minutes
Total: 30-40 minutes

Pressure Level: High
Release: 10-minute natural
Makes: About 2 cups

Ingredients

1½ cups ketchup (preferably an unsweetened brand, like Westbrae Natural® organic unsweetened ketchup)
⅓ cup apple cider vinegar
⅓ cup soy sauce
¼ cup Worcestershire sauce
3 garlic cloves (preferably roasted)
1 teaspoon dry mustard powder
2 tablespoons yellow mustard
½ teaspoon black pepper
½ cup onion, minced
1 teaspoon garlic salt
¼–½ teaspoon crushed red pepper flakes

> This barbecue sauce is full flavored and holds up to any use. Try it as the sauce on a pizza and top with shredded chicken, slices of onion, mozzarella cheese, and pineapple.

> For a sweeter sauce, add ¼ cup of honey or 7 pitted dates to the sauce before cooking.

Directions

1. Add all of the ingredients to the pressure cooker pot and stir well. Secure the lid and turn pressure release knob to a sealed position. Cook at high pressure for 15 minutes.

2. When cooking is complete, use a natural release for 10 minutes and then release any remaining pressure.

3. Blend until smooth with an immersion blender or in a regular blender. Use immediately or transfer to glass jars and refrigerate for up to 2 weeks. Also freezes very well in freezer-safe resealable bags.

Use leftovers over cooked pasta for a quick mac and cheese, as a substitute for pizza sauce (YUM!), poured over roasted veggies, drizzled on top of chili . . . I could go on forever!

Butternut Squash Nacho Cheese Sauce

I never had any intention of putting this cheese sauce in this book. I made it long before I ever used it for the burrito discussed on page 55 and have used it often for things like mac and cheese, nachos, salad dressing (I know that sounds strange, but think taco salad!), and roasted veggies. So consider this recipe a "How to cook butternut squash in the pressure cooker" guide, and the cheese sauce is an incredible bonus use for that there squash. The 25-minute cook time works perfectly for spaghetti squash as well. Enjoy!

Prep: 10 minutes
Pressure: 8 minutes for chopped squash;
25 minutes for whole
Total: 25 minutes for chopped squash;
50 minutes for whole

Pressure Level: High
Release: Quick for chopped squash;
10-minute natural for whole
Makes: About 4 cups

Ingredients

4–5 cups chopped butternut squash or 1 medium-whole butternut squash

3 tablespoons butter

¼ cup chopped onion

2 cloves garlic, minced

4 tablespoons whole wheat flour (can substitute white flour)

2 cups almond cashew milk (can substitute with any type of milk)

1½ cups shredded extra sharp cheddar cheese

¼ cup nutritional yeast (can omit, but it adds a great "cheesy" flavor)

4–6 pickled jalapeño slices (add more or less to adjust heat)

2 tablespoons liquid from jalapeño jar

1 teaspoon Dijon mustard

1 teaspoon cumin

1 teaspoon paprika

1 teaspoon chili powder

1 teaspoon kosher salt

Directions

1. Add 1 cup of water to the pressure cooker pot and place collapsible steamer basket inside. Place chopped squash on top. Secure the lid and turn pressure release knob to a sealed position. Cook at high pressure for 8 minutes. If using a whole squash, place the squash on top of a trivet and cook at high pressure for 25 minutes.

2. For chopped butternut squash, when cooking is complete, use a quick release. For whole squash, use a natural release for 10 minutes and then release any remaining pressure (could also use a full natural release). Remove the peel with your hands or a knife, scrape out seeds, and coarsely chop.

3. While squash is cooking, add butter to a small pot and melt on the stove top over medium-high heat. Add onion and garlic and stir until softened, about 4 minutes. Sprinkle flour on top of onions and stir for 1 minute. Slowly pour in milk and whisk constantly until it thickens, 2–3 minutes. Pour mixture into a blender and add cooked butternut squash, cheese, nutritional yeast (if using), jalapeño slices and liquid, mustard, cumin, paprika, chili powder, and salt. Blend until smooth.

4. Use immediately or store in an airtight container in the fridge for up to 2 weeks.

Cranberry Apple Sauce

In my world, the only reason turkey is a star at any holiday table is because of the cranberry sauce that accompanies it. My grandma, bless her sweet soul, was famous for dry, bland turkey, but next to a blob of her famous Jell-O®-like cranberry sauce (I didn't know or care at the time that it came from a can), it was one of my favorite things to eat. Now that I'm all grown up and have made—count 'em—two delicious Thanksgiving turkeys, it was time to master an amazing chunky cranberry sauce. So I did, with my pressure cooker no less. With the combination of orange juice, apple cider, maple syrup, and a Honeycrisp apple, this cranberry sauce is a perfect balance of tart and sweet and is heavenly on turkey. But since there's always leftover cranberries (because apparently I'm the only one that eats turkey and cranberry sauce with a spoon like it's soup), this sauce is divine on toast and pancakes and stirred into homemade yogurt.

Prep: 10 minutes
Pressure: 5 minutes
Total: 20 minutes

Pressure Level: High
Release: 5-minute natural
Makes: About 2 cups

Ingredients

12 ounces fresh or frozen cranberries, rinsed
zest and juice of 1 large orange
1 Honeycrisp apple, peeled, cored, and chopped
½ cup apple cider
½ cup pure maple syrup

Directions

1. Add all of the ingredients to the pressure cooker pot and stir well. Secure the lid and turn pressure release knob to a sealed position. Cook at high pressure for 5 minutes.

2. When cooking is complete, use a natural release for 5 minutes and then release any remaining pressure. If liquid sprays while releasing the pressure, quickly turn the valve to the sealed position and wait 5 more minutes.

3. Simmer for 2-3 minutes to thicken. Sauce will thicken further as it cools. Serve warm, or can also be made up to a week in advance and stored in the fridge. Freezes very well.

Marinara Sauce

Whenever I see a bottle of marinara sauce, I have flashbacks of my twin pregnancy. I don't know which nutrient I was lacking, but for several weeks, nothing sounded better than eating marinara sauce straight out of the jar, with a long spoon or a smoothie straw. Trust me, I know how gross that sounds, but this homemade pressure cooker marinara sauce . . . it's deep, rich tomato flavor is dreamy on pasta, meatball subs, spaghetti, breadsticks, basically everything. Totally smoothie straw-worthy.

Prep: 2 minutes
Pressure: 15 minutes
Total: 25 minutes

Pressure Level: High
Release: Natural
Makes: 3-4 cups

Ingredients

1 teaspoon olive oil
2 roasted garlic cloves, finely chopped
28-ounce can crushed tomatoes
1 small bay leaf
1 teaspoon dried oregano
kosher salt and freshly ground black pepper
2 tablespoons chopped fresh basil

> Use for everything from pasta to pizza. This recipe also doubles in the pressure cooker very well.

Directions

1. Select sauté and add olive oil. Add garlic and sauté until golden. Turn off pressure cooker, add crushed tomatoes, bay leaf, oregano, and a big pinch of kosher salt and pepper; stir. Secure the lid and turn pressure release knob to a sealed position. Cook at high pressure for 15 minutes.

2. When cooking is complete, use a natural release.

3. Stir in fresh basil. Sauce can be stored in a container in the fridge for up to 2 weeks or in the freezer in a freezer-safe resealable bag for several months.

Teriyaki Sauce

I felt like I had struck gold when I tasted this sauce. It had all the sweetness of teriyaki sauce that makes it so special, but it's 100% naturally sweetened. My kids looked at me in horror when they peered inside the pot and saw what they thought were big bugs (perfect time for the "It's not what's on the outside, but what's on the inside that counts" conversation). Those "bugs" were, of course, the dates, and they are what makes this over-the-top teriyaki sauce so fabulous. Enjoy in teriyaki bowls, full of vegetables and rice, or brushed on chicken and pineapple, cooked on the grill.

Prep: 5 minutes
Pressure: 5 minutes
Total: 20 minutes

Pressure Level: High
Release: 5-minute natural
Makes: About 2 cups

Ingredients

15 Medjool dates, pitted
¾ cup reduced-sodium soy sauce
¼ cup white wine vinegar
3 cloves garlic, preferably roasted
1 tablespoon grated fresh ginger
½ cup chicken broth

Peel ginger and store it in a small resealable freezer bag. It will last for months and grates much easier frozen.

Directions

1. Add all ingredients to the pressure cooker pot. Secure the lid and turn pressure release knob to a sealed position. Cook at high pressure for 5 minutes.

2. When cooking is complete, use a natural release for 5 minutes and then release any remaining pressure.

3. Carefully ladle into a blender or into a food processor bowl. Blend until very smooth, 1–2 minutes. Can be used as a marinade, sauce for vegetables, meat glaze, and rice bowls.

If your grocery store has an olive or salad bar, look for roasted garlic in olive oil. If you're not a fan of raw garlic, peeling garlic, or want to find a way to store garlic that will contain the smell, this is the best food hack ever! Buy a spoonful and store in the freezer. It thaws within a few minutes on the counter and can be used for any recipe that asks for garlic.

Zucchini Pesto Sauce

Never in my years as a mother have I seen my kids eat so much of a green food; that's just how good this sauce is. Recipes like this remind me that food can be good with only a few ingredients. Less can definitely be more. Mix it into rice, pour it over pasta, or—my personal favorite—smother on tomato-garlic bread.

Prep: 5 minutes
Pressure: 5 minutes
Total: 15 minutes

Pressure Level: High
Release: 10-minute natural
Makes: 6-7 cups

Ingredients

1 tablespoon olive oil
1 cup coarsely chopped onion
2 garlic cloves (preferably roasted)
5 medium zucchini, roughly chopped
2 teaspoons salt
¾ cup water
1 cup packed basil leaves

> Serve with toast! I like to spread ricotta cheese on toast, add a sprinkle of kosher salt and freshly cracked pepper, then drizzle this sauce over the top, and eat it with a fork and knife. Try spreading garlic butter on toast, topping it with tomatoes and pepper jack; brown it under the broiler, and drizzle with this Zucchini Pesto Sauce. Now that's fancy!

Directions

1. Select sauté on the pressure cooker and add olive oil. When hot, add chopped onion and garlic; sauté until soft, about 3-4 minutes. Add the zucchini, salt, and water; stir. Secure the lid and turn pressure release knob to a sealed position. Cook at high pressure for 5 minutes.

2. When cooking is complete, use a natural release for 10 minutes and then release any remaining pressure.

3. Add basil to the pot. Either use an immersion blender directly in the pot or pour into a blender; blend until completely smooth. Store in a container in the refrigerator for up to 2 weeks, or in a freezer-safe resealable bag in the freezer for several months.

Savory Sun-dried Tomato Pesto Cheesecake with Mixed Greens and Tomato Vinaigrette

My most favorite flavor combination is also one of the most classic: tomato and basil. I so badly wanted to squeeze it into the book somewhere but really struggled to come up with an acceptable pressure cooker version. This match made in heaven finally found its place in the form of a cheesecake—go figure! I love savory cheesecakes. They're different, unexpected, and love at first bite. Serve it on a large bed of greens with a side of grilled chicken or steak and a large douse of Tomato Vinaigrette. Then just sit back and listen to the chorus of "yum" sounds as your family and friends experience the perfect bite of cheesecake, greens, meat, and dressing. Now let's have a moment of silence for this Tomato Vinaigrette. It takes seconds to whip up, and it is positively drinkable. Do NOT skip out on the vinaigrette (but if you must, a balsamic dressing is also delicious). It's always fun to bring something different to the party, and this cheesecake right here will be the dish of the night!

Prep: 15 minutes
Pressure: 20 minutes
Total: 50 minutes

Pressure Level: High
Release: 10-minute natural
Serves: 6–8 as a side

Ingredients

2 cups pretzels
3 tablespoons butter, melted
8 ounces whipped cream cheese, room temperature
2 eggs, room temperature
½ teaspoon salt
¼ cup pesto
¼ cup chopped sun-dried tomatoes
    (*not* jarred sun-dried tomatoes in oil)
¼ cup toasted pine nuts
mixed greens
cherry tomatoes, halved
roasted pine nuts to garnish

For Tomato Vinaigrette

14-ounce can of whole, peeled tomatoes, drained
¼ cup white wine vinegar
1 teaspoon kosher salt
1 teaspoon Dijon mustard
¼ cup extra virgin olive oil

Directions

1. **To make crust:** In a food processor or blender, pulse pretzels until coarsely chopped. Pour into a small bowl and stir in melted butter until incorporated throughout. Press the mixture onto the bottom and about ½-inch up the sides of a 7-inch springform pan. Place in freezer for at least 30 minutes. (This step can be done a few days in advance, if desired.)

2. **To make cheesecake filling:** In a medium mixing bowl, beat cream cheese, eggs, and salt until very smooth. Scrape the bowl and then add the pesto. Mix just until incorporated. Add sun-dried tomatoes and pine nuts and stir by hand to combine. Scrape cheese mixture into the crust; smooth the top.

3. Add 1 cup of water to the pressure cooker pot and place trivet inside. Carefully place the filled pan on the trivet. Secure the lid and turn pressure release knob to a sealed position. Cook at high pressure for 20 minutes.

4. When cooking is complete, use a natural release for 10 minutes and then release any remaining pressure.

5. Place the pan on a wire rack, blot any excess water from the top of the cheesecake with a paper towel, and cool for 10 minutes.

6. While the cheesecake is cooling, make the Tomato Vinaigrette by adding tomatoes, vinegar, salt, and Dijon mustard to the bowl of a food processor and blending until smooth. With the food processor still running, slowly stream in the olive oil and blend until it emulsifies. Taste and add more salt if needed. (Can be made up to a week in advance and stored in an airtight container in the fridge.)

7. After cheesecake has cooled slightly, carefully remove the springform ring. If it is sticking, run a knife around the edges to loosen the cake.

8. To serve, place mixed greens on a plate and top with cherry tomatoes and pine nuts. Place a slice of warm cheesecake next to the mixed greens and drizzle vinaigrette over everything.

9. The cheesecake can be served the day-of, either warm or at room temperature, or can be made one day in advance and eaten cold in the same manner.

It's an extra step, but prebaking the crust will keep a crunchier texture. After pressing the crust into the pan, place in a 350°F oven for 10 minutes. Cool completely before filling.

Frozen Whipped Cream Dollops:
Vanilla, Maple Cinnamon, and Peppermint

Heavy cream seems to be an ingredient I most often have leftovers of. The carton sits in my fridge, half full, until I see it's expired, and then it gets dumped, just in time for me to find another recipe that requires a drizzle of cream—and the process begins again. So that's problem one. Problem two is that my kids refuse to eat "soggy oatmeal" (definition: piping hot oatmeal drowning in a sea of cold milk in an attempt to quickly cool it down). Problem three: my kids find it preposterous to dilute their hot chocolate with cold milk but cry that they can't drink it without it burning their mouths. Well, consider problems 1, 2, and 3 solved! My leftover heavy cream will forever be transformed into these cute little Frozen Whipped Cream Dollops, and my kids buzz with excitement as they watch their dollop melt into a river of vanilla cream in their oatmeal and hot chocolate. So while I can't claim to have ever cured a disease, I feel proud to say that my kids think I'm a complete genius!

Prep: 1 minute
Total: 10 minutes
Makes: 50-60

Ingredients
1 quart heavy whipping cream
1-2 tablespoons vanilla extract
optional sweetener: 1-2 tablespoons
　　maple syrup or powdered sugar

Variations

Maple Cinnamon Whipped Cream Dollops
1 quart heavy whipping cream
4 teaspoons cinnamon
4 teaspoons vanilla extract
¼ cup pure maple syrup

Peppermint Whipped Cream Dollops
1 quart heavy whipping cream
4 teaspoons peppermint extract
⅓ cup powdered sugar

Directions

1. Add all ingredients to a blender. Blend at medium speed until thick. Alternatively you could use a hand mixer.

2. Cover a cookie sheet with nonstick foil or parchment paper and place heaping tablespoons of cream onto the pan. I use a small cookie scoop to make this process really fast.

3. Place in the freezer until very hard, at least 2 hours. Transfer to a gallon-sized resealable freezer bag and store in freezer for whenever there's a need to dress something up or cool something down with a delicious dollop of vanilla cream richness! (Think oatmeal, hot chocolate, French toast, on top of ice cream, etc.) Enjoy!

Homemade Ricotta Cheese

I never knew how much I loved ricotta until I made my own. Before that, it was merely the star ingredient in my mom's famous manicotti recipe (which she insists I mention is on the back of the manicotti box), and that's the only time I ever had it. Since making my own, this glorious creamy cloud of cheese goes on toast with blueberries and honey, in eggs for shockingly fluffy scrambled eggs, and in every baked good I can fold it into. The pressure cooker makes it so simple, I can make a fresh batch super quick any time I need it. As a busy working mom, I have to pick and choose which things I'll take time to make homemade, and this one definitely makes the list.

Note: *Instructions for the recipe are specific to the Instant Pot®, which has a yogurt/boil function. Some adjustments may be needed if using a different electric pressure cooker.*

Prep: 5 minutes
Total: 20-60 minutes

Pressure Level: Use Yogurt/Boil setting
Makes: About 2 cups ricotta cheese

Ingredients
½ gallon whole milk
1½ teaspoon salt
⅓ cup lemon juice

Directions

1. Add milk and salt to the pressure cooker pot. Secure the lid. Press the "Yogurt" function, then press "Adjust" until it says "Boil." This will warm the milk to about 180°F. When the boiling cycle is complete, remove the lid and place a thermometer in the milk. Select sauté to bring milk to 190°F, stirring often. (Can also use the slow-cook function to warm cold milk to 190°F if pressure cooker doesn't have the "Yogurt/Boil" function.)

2. When the milk reaches 190°F, unplug the pressure cooker and add the lemon juice. Give it a very gentle stir. The milk will start to separate immediately.

3. Let the pot of milk sit undisturbed for 10 minutes. The milk will separate into white, milky curds and watery, yellow-colored whey.

4. Without stirring it, pour the curds into either a colander lined with a double layer of cheesecloth, a nut milk bag, or yogurt strainer.

5. Let the ricotta drain for 10-60 minutes, depending on how thick you want it. If it becomes too thick, you can stir some of the whey back into the ricotta.

6. Scrape the ricotta into a bowl. It can be used right away or stored in an airtight container in the refrigerator for up to a week.

Tips
- Recipe can be successfully doubled.
- Distilled white vinegar can be used in place of the lemon juice, with very little change in the flavor.
- Don't throw away the whey! It can be used as a buttermilk substitute or in place of water in homemade bread.

Tips for Making Homemade Yogurt

Turn the page for my fail-proof homemade yogurt recipe.

While yogurt doesn't have anything to do with the pressurizing abilities of a pressure cooker, it is one of my absolute favorite things to make in it. Not all makes and models will have a "Yogurt" function, but I highly suggest you buy one that does. The pressure cooker makes the most creamy, dreamy, and mildly tangy yogurt ever! I know this for a fact because everyone I gift it to begs for more and eventually buys a pressure cooker! For the price of one gallon of milk and a yogurt starter, this recipe makes up to 3 quarts of yogurt and at least 1 quart of whey that can be used as a buttermilk substitute. After making yogurt in the pressure cooker a bazillion times, I've learned some new tips and tricks that I will share in this recipe.

First, a few notes to guarantee success:

- Here's what to expect timewise: 1 hour for milk to warm to 185°F, about 1½–2 hours to cool to 110°F, 8 hours of incubation, and then 6 hours or overnight refrigeration to chill yogurt in the pot before straining. The majority of this, of course, is inactive time on your part.
- This recipe is made with 2% milk. Lower to no-fat milk may be used, but will result in a thinner yogurt that isn't as smooth. Whole milk will result in more yogurt, less whey, and is very thick and creamy.
- The powdered milk is completely optional; it can help to create a thicker yogurt and boosts the amount of protein in the final product, but the yogurt is still wonderful without it.
- Warming the milk to 185°F will produce a thicker end product, more like Greek yogurt. I've also made my yogurt with the milk only reaching 165–175°F; it's a bit thinner, but it's still really good yogurt.
- Let the milk naturally cool to 110°F. In a pinch, the process can be hurried along by placing the pot in a sink full of ice water (this only takes about 20 minutes), but the yogurt tends to be smoother when allowed a gradual cool.
- Use a high quality, fresh starter that is unflavored. My favorite is Fage® Total 2%. I've also played around with using different amounts of starters and always come back to a quarter cup. My end product is thicker and smoother.
- Strain yogurt with a nut milk bag, cheesecloth, or—my favorite—the Euro Cuisine® yogurt strainer. A full gallon of milk requires either two nut milk bags or two strainers to do it all at once. After the 8-hour yogurt incubation is complete, leave the yogurt undisturbed and place it in the fridge overnight until completely chilled. This will thicken the yogurt even more, and your end product will be more yogurt and less whey. I strain it for 30–60 minutes, which is thick enough to sit on a spoon but doesn't hold its shape for long. Strain longer, even overnight, for a Greek yogurt consistency—just make sure to do this in the refrigerator. If yogurt ends up thicker than you'd like, simply add in a splash or two of whey and whisk to combine.
- If using sweetener or vanilla extract, add it after the yogurt has incubated, cooled, and strained. Always add pure vanilla extract after the incubation period to avoid disturbing the yogurt-making process (the alcohol can affect the consistency of your final product). If using an imitation vanilla (that is alcohol-free) or fresh vanilla beans, it can be added at any time (use about 1 tablespoon of vanilla extract—or scrape 1 vanilla bean—and about ½ cup sweetener like honey, pure maple syrup, agave, or white sugar).
- To use your own homemade yogurt as a starter, be sure to reserve one quarter cup. Use within a week for best results. If you're not going to be needing it that quickly, it can be frozen for up to 3 months. Thaw it gradually in the fridge, and it will work just as well as a fresh starter.
- Finally, a word on different pressure cookers. Some pressure cookers, like the Instant Pot®, have a "Boil" function that will ideally take it to 180–185°F and beep when it's complete. It won't always get quite to that temperature, but it's not completely necessary that it does. If the yogurt isn't coming out as thick as desired, try using the sauté function to simmer milk the rest of the way to 185°F. Other pressure cookers like the Fagor Lux use the slow-cook function to warm the milk to 185°F. Keep a thermometer close by, and near the end of 40 minutes, check to see when it reaches temperature. Stirring the milk periodically during this warming stage will help prevent milk from scorching on the bottom. However, from my experience, if I neglect to stir it, a thin brown layer does develop on the bottom of the pot, but the flavor is unaffected, so I consider stirring optional.

Homemade Yogurt

I've made a thousand batches of yogurt and can now offer my "fail-proof recipe." I can confidently say that there is no store-bought yogurt that can hold a candle to this creation. You are about to make a lot of people very happy by gifting them a pretty jar of this creamy, dreamy yogurt and a bag of homemade granola.

Prep: 5 minutes
Boil/Warm: About 1 hour
Incubate: 8 hours

Chill: 6 hours or overnight
Strain: 30–60 minutes
Makes: About 3 quarts

Ingredients
1 gallon 2% milk
3 tablespoons powdered milk (optional)
¼ cup plain yogurt with live and active cultures (I like Fage® Total 2%)
1–2 tablespoons vanilla extract (optional)
½ cup sweetener, such as pure maple syrup, agave, honey, or white sugar (optional)

Directions

1. Add milk to the pressure cooker pot. Whisk in powdered milk, if using.

2. Secure the lid and press the "Yogurt" function button. (Note: It doesn't matter what position the pressure release valve is in for yogurt making.) Press adjust until display reads "Boil." For pressure cookers that don't have the automatic boil function, simply use the slow-cook or sauté function to warm the milk to 185°F.

3. Remove the yogurt starter from the fridge and allow it to sit on the counter, until ready to use.

4. When "Boil" cycle is complete and milk has reached 185°F (this takes about an hour), remove pot from cooker and place on top of a cooling rack. Stir milk occasionally, until it cools to 110°F (this takes about 1½–2 hours).

5. When milk is 110°F, ladle 2–3 scoops into a bowl, add the yogurt starter, and whisk until smooth. Pour back into the pot, whisking until well incorporated.

6. Place pot back inside the base, secure the lid, press the "Yogurt" function, and adjust to incubate for 8 hours.

7. When "Yogurt" cycle is complete, place the pot of yogurt in the fridge to chill for about 6 hours (or overnight).

8. When chilled, divide yogurt into two nut milk bags and hang bags over the top of a large bowl to collect the whey. This can also be done with two yogurt strainer bowls (like the Euro Cuisine® Greek Yogurt Maker). Strain yogurt for 30–60 minutes or strain in the refrigerator overnight until it reaches desired thickness.

9. Return strained yogurt to a bowl and whisk until smooth if needed. Add pure vanilla extract and sweetener at this point, if desired. If yogurt is really thick, use a hand mixer to smooth and incorporate vanilla and/or sweetener.

10. Store in a yogurt strainer bowl (minus the strainer of course, like the Euro Cuisine® bowl) or in quart-sized mason jars topped with a tight-fitting lid. The yogurt will stay good in the fridge for up to 2 weeks. Save a quarter cup of the yogurt to use as a starter for the next batch of yogurt.

11. Serve cold. Topping possibilities are endless: fruit, honey, pure maple syrup, granola, etc.

Tips

- For an extra thick and creamy yogurt, let strain overnight. Use a hand mixer to whisk yogurt until smooth, adding a splash of whey if needed.
- Don't discard the whey! I like to fill quart-sized mason jars three-quarters full of whey, top off with yogurt, and shake to combine in order to make it thicker.
- Top with a mason jar pour-cap for easy pouring.
- Use the mixture as a buttermilk substitute in pancakes, waffles, muffins, etc.

FRUIT AND JAM

Chunky Apple Bowls

My favorite lunch consists of homemade yogurt, fruit, granola, coconut chips, and a dollop of almond butter. To my horror, I pulled out my yogurt container one day, to discover that one of my children had decided to hide their ham sandwich inside of it. Why? Do I even bother asking a 3-year-old for the reasoning? Probably not. My next thought was, "How bad could it be?" A second glance told me: bad, really bad. So it went down the drain along with my dreams of the perfect yogurt bowl for lunch. Now what? I scanned the fridge, and the Chunky Apple Bowl was born. And if I didn't love my homemade yogurt so much, this would be my #1 pick for lunch every day. So, it's second choice, and it's fantastic. The combination of creamy, crunchy, cold, and chewy (CCCC—did I just start a new food world acronym?) satisfies every time.

Prep: 5 minutes
Pressure: 1 minute
Total: 1 hour (includes chill time)

Pressure Level: High
Release: Quick
Serves: 1 (can be doubled or tripled)

Ingredients

1 large apple
½–1 cup unsweetened vanilla almond milk
1 tablespoon peanut butter or almond butter
1 tablespoon unsweetened toasted coconut (like
  Dang® coconut chips)
¼–½ cup granola, store-bought or homemade
1-2 tablespoons raisins

> Eat warm! Serve apples hot from the pressure cooker and top with warm milk and granola.

Directions

1. Chop apple into large bite-sized chunks. Spray an 8-inch perforated pan or a collapsible steamer basket with nonstick cooking spray and scatter the apple chunks inside. Set aside.

2. Add 1 cup of water to the pressure cooker pot and place trivet inside. Place pan on the trivet. Secure the lid and turn pressure release knob to a sealed position. Cook at high pressure for 1 minute.

3. When cooking is complete, use a quick release.

4. Carefully remove pan and place in refrigerator to chill apples. This can be done in large batches; the apples may be stored in a sealed container in the fridge until ready to use.

5. To prepare the bowls, place apples in the bowl, pour milk over the top, and add desired type of nut butter, coconut, granola, and raisins. Enjoy immediately.

> Double, triple, or even quadruple the number of apples. Use a variety of different apples. Using different kinds of apples creates more taste and texture in your bowl. Feel free to switch up the toppings as well!

Cinnamon Vanilla Applesauce

This applesauce right here is straight-up dessert! It's rich, silky, and bursting with flavor. Hot, straight out of the pot, a bowlful of this applesauce topped with granola and raisins is enough to make my kids put down their chocolate for a taste. Use it in your baked goods, and you'll have people wondering why their bread and muffins don't ever turn out as goods as yours. Aside from the pain of peeling and coring apples, it comes together easy peasy in a pressure cooker. And don't even get me started on the glorious smell that explodes into the room when the pressure is released through the valve. Yum!

Prep: 10 minutes
Pressure: 4 minutes
Total: 20 minutes

Pressure Level: High
Release: 5-minute natural
Makes: about 4 cups

Ingredients

10 large apples, peeled, cored, and quartered or sliced (Golden Delicious, Honeycrisp, Jonagold, etc., or a variety)
¼ cup apple cider or apple juice
2 teaspoons ground cinnamon
1 vanilla bean, split, seeds scraped from pod (do not discard seeds); may substitute 1 teaspoon vanilla extract

> Applesauce freezes well. Separate into freezer-safe containers and label. Thaw in the refrigerator.

Directions

1. Add apples, apple juice, cinnamon, and vanilla pod and seeds to the pressure cooker pot; stir to combine. Secure the lid and turn pressure release knob to a sealed position. Cook at high pressure for 4 minutes.

2. When cooking is complete, use a natural release for 5 minutes and then release any remaining pressure. For a thicker applesauce, use sauté feature to simmer until desired consistency is achieved.

3. Remove vanilla bean pod. Simply stir for a chunky applesauce; for a very smooth sauce, blend in pot with an immersion blender (or transfer to a blender).

> Homemade applesauce takes baked goods such as muffins and bread to a whole new flavor level!

Easy Pumpkin Butter

It seems everyone has their secret to what makes marriage work. My husband and I are VERY different (for example, I wake up at 3, he goes to bed at 3; he watches black-and-white movies, I watch reality TV cooking competitions). So here's my secret—make those opposites work for you! Especially when it comes to food. He eats the chicken from my curry; I get his veggies. I eat the salad toppings; he finishes off my lettuce. I eat the pizza toppings; he eats my crust. He eats the ice cream; I get his last bite of cone (which is basically saint status right there). He eats the pumpkin pie filling and leaves me the crust . . . until I met pumpkin butter—a.k.a. warm heaven in a jar. I've splattered pumpkin butter all over my stove top many, many times to have this goodness in my life, but no more! Making it in the pressure cooker infuses all the wonderful spices into the pumpkin puree so nicely and makes the dates so soft and puree-able. I'll say it again: pure warm heaven in a jar. Which brings me to tip number two for making marriage work: make pumpkin butter daily, then top it with crumbled pie crust and a dollop of cream . . . who can bicker with that on the table?! You are welcome.

Prep: 10 minutes
Pressure: 15 minutes
Total: 25 minutes

Pressure Level: High
Release: Quick
Makes: About 4 cups

Ingredients

29 ounces canned pumpkin
1 tablespoon vanilla extract
¾ cup apple cider or apple juice
8 pitted dates or ¾ cup brown sugar
3 cinnamon sticks
2 teaspoons pumpkin pie spice

> Stir pumpkin butter into unsweetened or vanilla yogurt, sprinkle with cinnamon, and use as a fruit dip.

Directions

1. To a heat-safe bowl, add pumpkin, vanilla, apple cider (or juice), dates (or brown sugar), cinnamon sticks, and pumpkin pie spice; stir, making sure the dates are immersed in the mixture. Set aside.

2. Add 1 cup of water to the pressure cooker pot and place trivet inside. Place bowl with pumpkin mixture on the trivet. Secure the lid and turn pressure release knob to a sealed position. Cook at high pressure for 15 minutes.

3. When cooking is complete, use a quick release.

4. Carefully remove bowl. Using a fork, remove cinnamon sticks from the hot pumpkin butter. Pour mixture into a blender and puree until completely smooth. This step can also be done directly in the bowl with an immersion blender. The dates will be moist and soft and will puree easily. If using brown sugar instead of dates, there is no need to puree; just stir until smooth.

5. Serve hot or cold on muffins, rolls, pancakes, etc. Store in an airtight container in the fridge for up to a week. Freezes very well.

Mango Sunshine Jam

When I see Ataúlfo mangos at the store in the early spring, I know I've made it through another winter and things are about to look up, hence the name Mango Sunshine. This jam is naturally sweet and bright and the perfect topping to hot homemade biscuits, toast, ice cream, cheesecake, and beyond.

Prep: 15 minutes
Pressure: 10 minutes
Total: 40 minutes

Pressure Level: High
Release: 10-minute natural
Makes: About 4 cups

Ingredients
6 cups very ripe mango, peeled and chopped
zest and juice of 1 orange
zest and juice of 1 lemon

Directions

1. Add all ingredients into a high powered blender. Purée until very smooth. Pour into the pressure cooker pot. Secure the lid and turn the pressure release knob to a sealed position. Cook at high pressure for 10 minutes.

2. When cooking is complete, use a 10-minute natural release.

3. If a thicker jam is desired, use sauté feature to simmer about 5 minutes.

4. Store in sealed containers in the fridge. Also freezes well.

Puréeing the fruit before it's cooked creates enough liquid, so there is no need to dilute your jam with water for the pressure cooker to come up to pressure. The result is a more concentrated mango flavor with plenty of sweetness. If even more sweetness is desired, add ½–1 cup of sugar when blending.

Peach Compote

When we moved into our new home, I became the owner of one glorious peach tree which produced more peaches than I had time to deal with. I needed something quick and easy to use up a lot of peaches. Behold: peach compote! For this peach compote recipe, I debated back and forth about dressing them up in cinnamon, vanilla, or sugar. But after two batches of glistening orange peach compote, I knew this recipe was meant to be all about the peaches. No sweetener, no spices, just let that peach flavor concentrate and shine with the magic of the pressure cooker!

Prep: 5 minutes
Pressure: 1 minute
Total: 10 minutes

Pressure Level: High
Release: 5-minute natural
Makes: About 2 cups

Ingredients

4 cups coarsely chopped peaches
1 tablespoon water
1 teaspoon vanilla extract
½ tablespoon cornstarch
1 tablespoon water

> Enjoy this peach compote over desserts, warm breakfasts, in yogurt, or simply by the spoonfuls.

Directions

1. Add peaches, water, and vanilla to the pot of the pressure cooker. Secure the lid and turn pressure release knob to a sealed position. Cook at high pressure for 1 minute.

2. When cooking is complete, use a natural release for 5 minutes and then release any remaining pressure.

3. To thicken, stir together cornstarch and water in a small bowl. Select sauté to bring peaches to a simmer. Pour cornstarch mixture into peaches and whisk continuously until thick, about 1 minute.

4. Use immediately, or cool and store in a sealed container in the fridge for up to a week. Can also be frozen to enjoy for months after peach season is over.

> The compote will thicken a bit as it cools, but if eating it hot, use a cornstarch slurry to thicken it up. Another option is to stir in a tablespoon of chia seeds while it's hot and cover for 5 minutes.

Unsweetened Fig Butter

Compared to my own kids, I was a seriously picky eater as a child. Hard candies, raisins, and berries of any variety made me shudder. But one of my biggest offenders: Fig Newtons. I thought they were old people cookies and that people ate them only because their teeth couldn't handle a crunchy cookie (wow, was I a brat as a child?). Ironically, one of the things I now love, just as much as I hated as a kid, are figs. Fresh, dried, and jammed, I just love the crunchy bits of seeds. So of course, I set out to make my own naturally sweet fig butter. It's thick, it's sweet, and it's jam-packed with crunch in every bite. And two out of my three kids 100% agree. The third child helped me make it and can't be convinced that the dates weren't big bugs.

Prep: 10 minutes
Pressure: 3 minutes
Total: 20 minutes

Pressure Level: High
Release: Quick
Makes: About 1 cup

Ingredients
15-20 dried figs (any variety will work)
2 large dates, pitted

Directions

1. Add figs and dates to the pressure cooker pot. Add enough water to cover them. Secure the lid and turn pressure release knob to a sealed position. Cook at high pressure for 3 minutes.

2. When cooking is complete, use a quick release.

3. Spoon figs and dates out of the pot. Press on them gently with another spoon to drain some of their excess liquid so as not to water down the flavor of the end product. Place them in the bowl of a food processor. Pulse until smooth, scraping down bowl if needed. Store in an airtight container in the fridge and use for toast, biscuits, a sandwich spread, or on a meat and cheese platter.

> This fig butter freezes very well so feel free to double or triple the recipe.

Infused Water

My two grocery store splurges are fresh ground almond butter and flavored water. The almond butter I justify quite easily—I REEAALLY like it. The flavored water is a little bit harder to justify. For one thing, it's water, and for another, it's twice the price of other bottled waters. Unfortunately, it's right across the aisle from my almond butter and calls to me over the noisy almond grinder. I often resist, get the rest of my groceries, head to the checkout stand, all the while thinking about that cold infused fruit water that is oh so refreshing. More times than not, I veer abruptly back towards the water and grab it before I can think any more about it. Just as I suspected, it's amazing, refreshing, and gone within 10 minutes. 'Cause, you know, it's not good if it's not ice cold. After seeing all the rage of at-home infused water, I had the genius idea to make my own in the pressure cooker, and it worked like magic. It is so potent in fact, that I only use about 2 tablespoons to flavor my water bottle. But let's not stop there! I freeze it into cubes and add that to my water bottle. Ice-cold infused water—for pennies! I'm gonna eat more almond butter now!

Prep: 5 minutes	**Pressure Level:** High
Pressure: 5 minutes	**Release:** Quick
Total: 15 minutes	**Makes:** About 1 quart

Ingredients
2-3 cups fruit, vegetables, and/or herbs of choice
4-6 cups water

Directions

1. Add fruit, vegetables, and/or herbs of choice to a mesh steamer basket. Place inside the pressure cooker pot. Add water to barely cover the produce, about 4-6 cups. Secure the lid and turn pressure release knob to a sealed position. Cook at high pressure for 5 minutes.

2. When cooking is complete, use a quick release.

3. Remove the steamer basket and discard cooked produce. Pour the flavored water into a mason jar to cool, then top with a lid and place in the refrigerator to chill.

4. Straight from the jar, the water is quite potent. I like to use 1-2 tablespoons per 8 ounces of water for just a slight hint of flavor; can sweeten if desired.

> If you don't have a mesh steamer basket, this could be made directly in the pot and then poured through a mesh strainer to filter out the produce, after it's cooked.

> Freeze flavored water in an ice cube tray and add 2-3 cubes to a bottle of water for cold flavored water on the go. The colorful ice cubes would also look gorgeous in a large punch bowl for a party.

INFUSED WATER VARIATIONS

There are hundreds of infused water recipes, but here are a few of my personal favorites:

Cucumber Mint
½ large cucumber, sliced
8 mint leaves

Grape Orange
2 cups grapes, sliced
1 orange, sliced

Cherry Lime
2 cups cherries, sliced
1 lime, sliced

Triple Citrus
1 large orange, sliced
1 lemon, sliced
1 lime, sliced

Mango Blueberry Vanilla
1 mango, chopped
½ cup blueberries, fresh or frozen
1 vanilla bean, split

Strawberry Lemon Basil
1 cup strawberries, sliced
1 lemon, sliced
6 basil leaves

Crio Bru™ Basic Recipe

For those of you that like to sleep in, I've got a secret for you. Early, EARLY mornings are the best time of day. Don't get me wrong—I love the time of day full of funny kid comments, cuddles, laughing, etc., but do you even know what you're sleeping through when you wait for the sun to come up? Peace. Total peace and quiet. The home is quiet, the world is quiet, my phone is quiet. It's in those serene, quiet moments that I can breathe freely. I can start a thought and actually finish it. It's heaven, my secret piece of heaven, that I'll sacrifice extra sleep for, any day. You know what makes it even better? A mug full of steaming hot Crio Bru.™ Crio Bru is basically cocoa beans brewed in the same manner as coffee. For years, I brewed it in a French press, which was kind of a pain, and waiting fifteen minutes to drink it was torture. On one of those quiet mornings, I got the idea to brew it in my pressure cooker, and you know what? I haven't touched my French press ever since. I make a big batch, strain it, store it in glass jars in my fridge, and my Crio Bru is now only two minutes away from being ready. Ease of preparation isn't the only thing that improved. The depth of flavor and color that my pressure cooker pulled out of those cocoa beans is straight-up mind-blowing. Even at half strength, it's stronger than the hundreds of cups I brewed throughout the years. I like to drink it in all of its deep, dark, unsweetened, pure chocolate glory, but it can be flavored and sweetened however you like. If I haven't convinced you of early mornings yet . . . well good. More quiet for me!

. . . .

Prep: 2 minutes
Pressure: 5 minutes
Total: 25 minutes

Pressure Level: High
Release: 10-minute natural
Serves: 4-6

. . . .

Ingredients

½ cup Crio Bru™ (any variety)
6 cups water
2 cups unsweetened vanilla almond milk (can substitute with any milk)
optional: Frozen Whipped Cream Dollop (page 189), vanilla extract, almond milk, creamer, cinnamon, honey, sugar, etc., to taste

> I don't drink coffee, but for those who do, I'm sure this method could work some serious magic on those beans as well.

Directions

1. Add Crio Bru, water, and milk to the pressure cooker pot. Secure the lid and turn pressure release knob to a sealed position. Cook at high pressure for 5 minutes.

2. When cooking is complete, use a natural release for 10 minutes and then release any remaining pressure.

3. Place a fine mesh sieve over a bowl and pour Crio Bru through the sieve to filter out the grounds. Be careful! The Crio Bru will be VERY hot.

4. Serve immediately with sweetener, if desired, and/or a Frozen Whipped Cream Dollop. This can also be stored in the refrigerator in a glass jar. Enjoy cold or pour into a microwave-safe mug and warm for 1-2 minutes.

> Typical brew time is about 15 minutes, but when it's sitting in your refrigerator brewed and ready, just 1-2 minutes in the microwave will get you a piping hot cup of super strong Crio Bru.

CRIO BRU VARIATIONS

For the following variations, add all of the ingredients and proceed with the basic directions on previous page.

Sweetened Crio Bru

½ cup Crio Bru
6 cups water
2 cups unsweetened vanilla almond milk (can substitute any type of milk)
⅓–½ cup sweetener (maple syrup, honey, agave, white sugar, brown sugar, etc.)

Pumpkin Spice Crio Bru

½ cup Crio Bru ground cocoa beans, pumpkin spice flavor (or any flavor will do)
6 cups water
2 cups milk (I use unsweetened vanilla almond milk)
⅓–½ cup pure maple syrup
½ cup pumpkin puree
2 teaspoons cinnamon
1 teaspoon vanilla extract

Peppermint Crio Bru

½ cup Crio Bru ground cocoa beans, peppermint flavor (or any flavor will do)
6 cups water
2 cups milk (I use unsweetened vanilla almond milk)
⅓–½ cup light agave
1 teaspoon vanilla extract
1–2 teaspoons peppermint extract

Wassail

The smell of wassail still brings me memories of pre-trick-or-treating excitement. However, as a child, when people talked about all the wonderful spices that were in wassail, I somehow interpreted that to mean it was spicy (in a hot sauce kind of way), and I don't believe I ever even tried wassail until I was an adult! What a shame! This particular wassail has warmed my family's hearts and bellies many of times, and we absolutely love it. Bonus: When you flip that pressure release knob, your house will be instantly filled with the most delightful, citrusy, spicy, apple-y, HEAVENLY smell known to mankind. Best Moment Ever!

Prep: 10 minutes
Pressure: 10 minutes
Total: 20 minutes

Pressure Level: High
Release: 10-minute natural release
Makes: 12 cups

Ingredients

8 cups apple cider
4 cups orange juice
5 cinnamon sticks
10 cloves
½ tsp nutmeg (preferably freshly grated)
zest and juice of 2 lemons
1 inch ginger, peeled
2 vanilla bean, split

Directions

1. Pour apple cider and orange juice into the pressure cooker pot. Place mesh steamer basket inside. Add cinnamon sticks, cloves, nutmeg, zest and juice of lemons, ginger, and vanilla beans to the basket. Secure the lid and turn pressure release knob to a sealed position. Cook at high temperature for 10 minutes.

2. When cooking is complete, use a 10-minute natural release.

3. Remove the steamer basket and discard its contents. Serve wassail hot from the pot. To keep the wassail warm and your house smelling amazing, turn the pressure cooker to warm or low slow-cook setting.

Infused Honey

More than once, I've found myself before a farm stand, gazing upon the many varieties of flavored honey, wondering how much money I could justify spending. It's not that I even wanted that many little jars of honey, I just NEEEEDED to know what they tasted like (like my son NEEEEDED to have his face painted by the sweet, young girl I could never say "no" to). So I'd pick a couple out, then a couple more, couple more, just to realize how much this was all going to cost, give myself a reality check, and put every single one back. Imagine how thrilled I was when the idea of infused honey crossed my mind. I made infused honey in my pressure cooker the very next day. And now I have a lazy Susan full of honeys of every flavor that cost a fraction of the market cost. Let your imagination go crazy here! I've included my favorites, but I'm sure there are many, many more amazing flavors that need to be discovered. And no, I will not be revealing to you or my husband how much money I've spent on my kids getting their faces painted. It's not important.

Prep: 5 minutes	**Pressure Level:** High
Pressure: 30-45 minutes	**Release:** Natural
Total: 60 minutes	**Makes:** About 1 cup

Ingredients

add-ins (see options on next page)
¾–1 cup honey (use a mild-tasting honey, not raw)

Directions

1. Place desired add-ins inside a half pint-sized mason jar. Cover with honey, leaving 1 inch of headspace. Stack 2 round coffee filters together and trim so it will hang over the jar about an inch. Place filters on top of the opening of the jar and screw a ring on tightly (just the ring, no flat needed).

2. Add 1 cup of water to the pressure cooker pot and place trivet inside. Place jar on the trivet. Secure the lid and turn pressure release knob to a sealed position. Cook at high pressure for 30 minutes (15 minutes for a more mild flavor).

3. When cooking is complete, use a natural release.

4. Carefully remove the mason jar (the honey will be HOT!). Using hot pads or a rag, remove the lid and vigorously stir the honey to infuse maximum flavor. Pour honey through a small, fine mesh sieve placed over another half pint-sized mason jar. Discard add-ins. (Honey can also be poured through cheesecloth.) Store at room temperature in a mason jar with a pourable lid for easy pouring.

INFUSED HONEY VARIATIONS

Lemon Ginger Honey
1 teaspoon dried lemon peel
4 cubes crystallized ginger
This version is even stronger with fresh lemon peel and fresh, peeled slices of ginger (see tips below). Great for a cough.

Elderberry Honey
¼ cup dried elderberries
Spoonful a day may keep cold and flu season away!

Cinnamon Honey
5 cinnamon sticks
To die for on whole wheat rolls right from the oven!

Lavender Honey
2 tablespoons dried lavender
Amazing drizzled over vanilla ice cream or yogurt.

Sweet Heat Honey
2 tablespoon crushed red pepper flakes
Drizzle over popcorn chicken or chicken wings.

Vanilla Honey
2-4 vanilla beans split or chopped
Dreamy stirred into hot drinks.

Chocolate Honey
2 tablespoons cocoa
Makes the best peanut butter-honey-banana sandwich ever!

Other ideas:
Dried mint, dried or fresh cranberries, roasted garlic, dried or fresh orange peel, rosemary, etc.

Tips
- I recommend using dried ingredients (not fresh) to flavor the honey if long-term storage is desired. If using fresh ingredients like citrus peels, herbs, etc., use within a month and store in the fridge.
- A 6-quart pressure cooker pot can fit up to 6 half pint-sized mason jars at a time.
- Don't make the honey without the coffee filters. They are there to keep extra moisture out of the honey.
- If making multiple flavors in a single batch, consider strong smells that may cross over into the other jars (for example, don't infuse a garlic honey next to a vanilla honey).
- Pour the honey through a fine mesh strainer when it's still warm for easier straining.
- Serve several choices of honey on a fancy platter with a mix of meat, cheese, and bread.
- Don't use expensive raw honey for this; you don't want to be exposing that precious gold to such high temperatures.

Alcohol smell may be strong
at first but will diminish
over a week or two. If still
overpowering at that point,
return to the pressure cooker for
another 30 minutes.

When vanilla extract is gone, let
the beans air dry, then add to
sugar for vanilla-infused sugar.

Vanilla Extract

Homemade vanilla extract always sounded so fancy to me, and I idolized people that could make something so miraculous . . . like, who are these people?! Are they secretly of royal descent? Do they have rich relatives in Africa supplying them with vanilla beans? How can I be one of these people! Obviously, I knew nothing about making vanilla, but when I discovered what it took, I thought, "I have to wait 4-6 months!" My family would be the first to tell you, I'm not exactly a patient person. So my pressure cooker–obsessed brain thought, "Could it be done?" Yes, yes it can. With only 30 minutes of pressure, my clear-colored vodka turned golden, and my kitchen smelled of sweet vanilla. Seriously, this vanilla is so good, the liquor store owner offered to buy his vodka back! I experimented with 4 different vodkas, rum, bourbon, and food-grade glycerin (for an alcohol-free version) and narrowed my favorites down to a mid-grade vodka and the glycerin. I prefer the glycerin version in uncooked foods like ice cream and whipped cream, and I use my vodka version mostly for cooked foods like cookies, jams, and pancakes. Vanilla beans are much cheaper in bulk, so buy a bunch and make extra batches of extract to share with friends and family.

CAUTION: *This method is NOT intended to be used with a stove top pressure cooker. Only use in an electric pressure cooker with a FULL NATURAL RELEASE. Keep electric pressure cooker away from any open flame while making vanilla with alcohol.*

NOTE: *This process is NOT designed for canning vanilla. The lid and ring are simply in place to keep a lot of the alcohol from dissipating.*

Prep: 10 minutes
Pressure: 30 minutes
Total: About 50 minutes
(plus an overnight rest before opening the jar)

Pressure Level: High
Release: Natural
Makes: About 2 cups

Ingredients
6–10 grade B Madagascar vanilla beans
About 2 cups Smirnoff® vodka 80 proof (40% alcohol)
  or food-grade vegetable glycerin

> The pressure cooker will fit up to three jars at a time, so feel free to double or triple the recipe.

Directions

1. Using a sharp-pointed knife or kitchen shears, cut each bean in half and then split in half lengthwise, leaving about an inch still connected. If beans are too dry to split, cut them into 1-inch pieces.

2. Place the vanilla beans in a pint-sized mason jar and add vodka or glycerin, leaving 1 inch of headspace. Top with a canning lid and ring and barely tighten.

3. Add 1 cup of water to the pressure cooker pot and place trivet inside. Put the mason jar on the trivet. Secure the lid and turn pressure release knob to a sealed position. Cook at high pressure for 30 minutes.

4. When cooking is complete, use a natural release.

5. Carefully remove the mason jar, swirl it lightly to release more vanilla seeds from the pod, and place on a cooling rack overnight.

6. Once cooled, top with a pourable lid and use in all your favorite recipes that call for vanilla extract.

Elderberry Syrup

I've seen my husband cry ONE time in the several years that we've been married. And it wasn't when he proposed, when I said "I do," when he broke his nose, when he kissed me good-bye while I left for a medical mission in Ghana, or even when he held his newborn babies. Nope, this tough guy had to be dragged to the ground under the grips of influenza, suffering from fever and body aches for two weeks before I saw him finally lose all control . . . for like 30 seconds anyways. But I was so shocked, I just stared and wondered to myself, what does a good wife do when a man falls like this? She sedates him with medication and whips him up some homemade elderberry syrup is what she does! So my idea for the syrup came about a year later, but better late than never, right?! Homemade elderberry syrup is remarkably affordable compared to the store-bought version full of sugar and preservatives and takes mere minutes to make. Now we can all do a little more to keep our families healthy (and our husbands manly) without maxing out our credit cards!

For those who aren't familiar with Elderberry Syrup and its uses, studies of elderberry, also known as Sambucus nigra, suggest that routine usage of elderberry may boost the immune system, help prevent minor illnesses, and decrease the severity and duration of symptoms when illness occurs. My intent here is not to offer medical advice or a cure for illness. I will always encourage visits and discussions with your physician to determine the best course of action for your individual situation and illness.

Prep: 5 minutes
Pressure: 10 minutes
Total: 25 minutes

Pressure Level: High
Release: Natural
Makes: 4-5 cups

Ingredients

1 cup dried elderberries
4 cups water
1 cinnamon stick (optional)
1 inch of fresh ginger, peeled (optional)

5 cloves (optional)
1 vanilla bean, split (optional)
¾-1 cup honey (preferably raw honey)

Directions

1. Add elderberries, water, and other desired optional ingredients to the pressure cooker pot and stir. Secure the lid and turn pressure release knob to a sealed position. Cook at high pressure for 10 minutes. When cooking is complete, use a natural release.

2. Set a fine mesh strainer over a bowl and pour the pot's contents into the strainer. Press on the elderberries to remove all of the juice. Discard the elderberries.

3. Allow the juice to cool completely, then whisk in ¾ cup honey. Add more honey to taste. Store in refrigerator for up to 2 weeks in mason jars with a pourable lid. Can also be frozen if longer storage is needed.

4. For adults, take 1-2 tablespoons each day; for children older than 1, take 1-2 teaspoons each day. Increase to 3-4 times per day if illness occurs. Do not give to children less than 1 year of age.

Perfect Brown Butter

This recipe hardly makes sense for a pressure cooker—the cooker doesn't even come to pressure. All I know is that if I add a cube of butter to the pot and set it for 2 minutes, my butter is transformed. I've made brown butter on the stove top, and it's really not all that complicated, but this pressure cooker method makes it even easier and consistently perfect every time. Plus, it's gonna give you rock-star status when friends and family just can't figure out how to make cookies taste as delectable as yours.

Important to note: *This has only worked successfully for me in the Instant Pot®.*

Prep: 1 minute
Pressure: 2 minutes
Total: 5 minutes

Pressure Level: High
Release: Quick
Makes: ½ cup

Ingredients
½ cup cold salted butter

Directions

1. Add butter to the pressure cooker pot. Secure the lid and turn pressure release knob to a sealed position. Cook at high pressure for 2 minutes.

2. When cooking is complete, use a quick release (there may not be any built-up pressure when it beeps; that's okay, just remove the lid and proceed to the next step).

3. Quickly remove the pan and swirl the butter inside the pot until the butter is golden yellow with brown flecks collected in the bottom. Immediately pour into a container to cool.

Brown butter adds extra depth of flavor to cookies, pancakes, muffins, popcorn, etc. When it's this easy to make, you can have it on hand for every one of those "secret ingredient" kind of situations.

Perfect Hard Boiled Eggs + Mama's Egg Salad Sandwich

My mom makes the best egg salad sandwich. However, it's only the best when she makes it. She insists there isn't a secret ingredient that she's not telling me about, so I guess it's just love. Or perhaps, it's the absolute joy of watching someone else make food for me. Whatever it is, my mom is always much more willing to make me an egg salad sandwich if I bring her the hard boiled eggs. Since the pressure cooker makes this process so easy, I say, "Oh yes I will!" I'm proudly including the egg salad sandwich recipe, created by my mother, the strongest, most powerful woman I know. She has raised some good kids. She's helped me through a lot of tough times and has been willing to listen through all of the happy, sad, and stressful moments. She's blunt, she's honest, and I love her like crazy. I'll refrain from adding "Love" to the list of ingredients, but just know, it's a mandatory element.

Prep: 1 minute
Pressure: 5 minutes
Total: 20 minutes

Pressure Level: High
Release: 5-minute natural
Makes: As many as you like!

Ingredients
Eggs (a dozen or so)

Directions

1. Add 1 cup of water to the pressure cooker pot and place collapsible steamer basket inside. Add eggs to the basket. Secure the lid and turn pressure release knob to a sealed position. Cook at high pressure for 5 minutes.

2. When cooking is complete, use a 5-minute natural release.

3. Prepare a bowlful of ice and cold water. After natural release, quickly transfer cooked eggs to the ice bath until cooled, about 10 minutes. Store eggs in refrigerator until ready to use.

Mama's Egg Salad Sandwich
(i.e.: the only egg salad sandwich, I ever wanna eat)
Makes 2–3 sandwiches

Ingredients
5 hardboiled eggs, peeled and roughly chopped
⅛ cup mayonnaise with olive oil
1 teaspoon yellow or Dijon mustard
big pinch of kosher salt
freshly cracked black pepper
¼ cup chopped sweet pickles
paprika

Directions

1. Mash eggs, mayonnaise, and mustard together in a bowl with a fork or potato masher, until desired consistency is achieved. Add salt, pepper, and pickles; stir.

2. Spread egg mixture on a slice of whole wheat bread and top with a second slice of bread. Can also be served open-face on a piece of whole wheat toast, with a sprinkle of paprika on top.

Ripening a Banana

I rarely have perfectly ripe bananas around because the second I see them ripening, they get chopped up and frozen for my kids' chocolate-banana-peanut butter smoothie obsession. When it comes time to make banana bread or Cami's scrumptious ricotta muffins, I usually have bright yellow, almost green bananas sitting on the counter. But when I need a ripe banana for baking, I need it now! Pressure cooker to the rescue! I've baked bananas in the oven, stuffed with chocolate chips, almond butter, etc., and they are always super sweet, almost syrupy. Curious, I threw some in the pressure cooker to see what would happen, and it worked like a charm. The pressure cooker takes them from unripe to soft, sweet, and bathed in syrup in minutes. Use them for baking, or dump them in a bowl and eat them with a spoon. Either way is a win!

Prep: 2 minutes
Pressure: 15 minutes
Total: 20 minutes

Pressure Level: High
Release: Quick
Makes: 4 bananas

Ingredients

4 unripe, small, unpeeled bananas (works best on bananas that are partially green or bright yellow with no brown spots)

Directions

1. Cut each banana lengthwise through the peel, about a half-inch deep, leaving a half-inch uncut at both ends. Add 1 cup of water to the pressure cooker pot and place trivet inside. Use a piece of foil to create a basket to sit on top of the trivet to collect any of the banana juices. For a sturdier surface, line an 8-inch perforated pan with foil and place it on top of the trivet, followed by the bananas, slit-side up. Secure the lid and turn pressure release knob to a sealed position. Cook at high pressure for 15 minutes.

2. When cooking is complete, use a quick release.

3. Let bananas cool slightly and then scrape from the peel, into a bowl, making sure to include any of the sweet, syrup-like juices that have collected in the foil. Mash bananas until smooth. They are now super sweet and ready to use in banana bread, muffins, etc.

> To turn this into a healthy and easy dessert, slice the bananas lengthwise and fill with toppings such as peanut butter, honey, jam, chocolate chips, nuts, etc. and cook as directed. For an extra special treat, top with caramel ice cream!

> Use mashed bananas to make banana frozen yogurt! Combine 1 cup of chilled, mashed banana, 1 cup of plain or vanilla yogurt, 1 cup of milk (any kind), and sweetener if desired (it's reminiscent of a banana-cream-pie shake even without any sweetener). Pour into ice cream maker and churn for 20–30 minutes. It's best eaten immediately, but it can also be stored in the freezer. Let sit at room temperature for 10 minutes to soften before serving.

Ripening an Avocado + Guacamole

My earliest memory of avocados was watching in horror as my dad cut one in half, removed the stone, and then ate the whole thing right out of the shell. What once made me cringe and gag as a kid now makes my mouth water in delight! The first time I actually used an avocado, it was rock hard, and I couldn't figure out why my guacamole looked more chopped than mashed. I now use avocados as much as possible for guacamole, salad dressings, smoothies, sandwich toppings, salads, etc. and could open one with my eyes closed. Avocados can take days to ripen, which has put me in a bind several times. So on a whim one day, I threw a rock-hard avocado into the pressure cooker. In less than 20 minutes, I was ready to make some guac! The texture is slightly different and is most ideal for mashing or blending, but I've chopped it up and eaten it in a salad and still really enjoyed it. An added benefit of quick-ripening an avocado in the pressure cooker is that it doesn't brown for days; I have had guacamole stay green for a week in the refrigerator! Typically they brown within hours of opening, despite all the tricks I've tried. This fabulous fruit (seriously, it's a fruit) just got even better!

Prep: 1 minute
Pressure: 10-15 minutes
Total: 20 minutes

Pressure Level: High
Release: Quick
Makes: As many avocados as you can fit in a single layer

Ingredients
unripe avocados

Directions

1. Add 1 cup of water to the pressure cooker pot and place trivet inside. Wrap desired number of avocados individually in tinfoil. Put wrapped avocados on the trivet in a single layer. Secure lid in place and turn pressure release knob to a sealed position. Cook at high pressure for 10 minutes.

2. When cooking is complete, use a quick release.

3. Unwrap the avocado. The avocado should be soft all over. If there are any areas that still feel firm, rewrap the avocado and return it to the rack with the firm side facing down; cook at high pressure for another 5 minutes followed by a quick release.

Guacamole
Makes 2-3 cups

Ingredients
2 medium-ripe avocados
¼ cup finely chopped onion
¼ cup finely chopped cilantro
juice of 1–2 limes
kosher salt to taste
1 jalapeño pepper, finely minced, seeded, and ribbed for a mild heat level

Directions

1. Mash the flesh of the avocados in a bowl. Stir in onion, cilantro, lime juice, salt, and jalapeño; continue to mash or whip until smooth or until desired consistency is reached. Taste and add more lime juice, salt, and/or pepper if necessary. Serve with tortilla chips.

PRESSURE COOKING CHARTS

(These guidelines are provided courtesy of Fagor America.)

Pressure cooking times are approximate times. Use these cooking times as a general guideline. Size and variety will alter cooking times.

Pressure Cooking Fruits (Fresh or Dried)

To achieve best results when pressure cooking dried or fresh fruit, please refer to these tips and hints:

1. Quick-release method is recommended when pressure cooking fruit to prevent overcooking.
2. A ½ cup of water is sufficient for cooking any quantity of fruit because the cooking time is very short.
3. Add sugar to fruit only after it is cooked, not before.

Fruit	Pressure Setting	Fresh (Cooking Time)	Dried (Cooking Time)
Apples, slices or chunks	High	2 minutes	3 minutes
Apples, whole	High	3 minutes	4 minutes
Apricots, whole or halved	High	2-3 minutes	3-4 minutes
Peaches	High	2-3 minutes	4-5 minutes
Pears	High	2-4 minutes	3-5 minutes
Plums/Prunes	High	2-4 minutes	3-5 minutes
Grapes/Raisins	High	1-2 minutes	4-5 minutes

Pressure Cooking Vegetables (Fresh or Frozen)

To achieve best results when pressure cooking fresh or frozen vegetables, please refer to these tips and hints:

1. Use the STEAM function when making steamed vegetable dishes.
2. Use the quick-release method when pressure cooking vegetables to prevent overcooking.
3. Use a minimum of 1 cup of liquid when cooking vegetables.
4. When steaming vegetables, use a stainless steel steamer basket and trivet.

Vegetable	Pressure Setting	Fresh (Cooking Time)	Frozen (Cooking Time)
Acorn Squash, chunks	High	6-7 minutes	8-9 minutes
Artichoke, 4 medium-large	High	8-10 minutes	10-12 minutes
Asparagus	High	1-2 minutes	2-3 minutes
Beets, whole, medium-large	High	20-25 minutes	25-30 minutes
Broccoli, florets	High	2-3 minutes	3-4 minutes
Brussel Sprouts	High	3-4 minutes	4-5 minutes
Butternut Squash, chunks	High	8-10 minutes	10-13 minutes
Cabbage, quartered	High	3-4 minutes	4-5 minutes
Carrots, whole or chunk	High	2-3 minutes	3-4 minutes
Cauliflower, florets	High	2-4 minutes	3-5 minutes
Celery, chunks	High	2 minutes	3 minutes
Collard Greens	High	4-5 minutes	5-6 minutes
Corn on the cob	High	3-5 minutes	4-6 minutes
Edamame, in pod	High	4-5 minutes	5-6 minutes
Eggplant	High	2 minutes	3 minutes
Endive	High	1-2 minutes	2-3 minutes
Kale, coarsely chopped	High	1-2 minutes	2-3 minutes
Leeks	High	2-4 minutes	3-5 minutes
Onions, sliced	High	2 minutes	3 minutes
Potatoes, whole, small	High	5-8 minutes	6-9 minutes
Potatoes, whole, large	High	10-12 minutes	11-13 minutes
Potatoes, sliced or cubed	High	5-8 minutes	6-9 minutes
Pumpkin, chunks	High	4-8 minutes	6-12 minutes
Spinach	High	1-2 minutes	3-5 minutes
Sweet Potatoes, cubed	High	7-9 minutes	9-11 minutes
Sweet Potatoes, whole	High	10-15 minutes	12-19 minutes
Tomatoes, quartered	High	2 minutes	4 minutes
Zucchini	High	2 minutes	3 minutes

Pressure Cooking Beans and Legumes (Dried or Soaked)

To achieve best results when cooking with dried or soaked beans/legumes, please refer to these tips and hints:

1. Rinse dried beans/legumes under cold water and drain; discard any pebbles or other debris in batch.
2. Do not fill cooker more than halfway to allow for beans/legumes to expand in size.
3. Use enough liquid to cover the beans/legumes.
4. Do not salt beans/legumes. Using salt while cooking the beans/legumes will prevent them from cooking properly.
5. Add 1-2 tablespoons of oil to beans/legumes to minimize frothing.
6. For best results, use the natural release method when cooking dried beans/legumes.

Beans and Legumes	Pressure Setting	Dried (180 ml cups) (Cooking Time)	Soaked Overnight (Cooking Time)
Adzuki Beans	High	20-25 minutes	10-15 minutes
Black Beans	High	20-25 minutes	10-15 minutes
Black-Eyed Peas	High	20-25 minutes	10-15 minutes
Cannellini Beans	High	35-40 minutes	20-25 minutes
Chestnuts, pierced	High	7-10 minutes	5-7 minutes
Chickpeas (Garbanzo Beans)	High	34-40 minutes	20-25 minutes
Great Northern Beans	High	28-30 minutes	23-25 minutes
Kidney Beans	High	25-30 minutes	20-25 minutes
Lentils (Brown)	High	15-20 minutes	N/A
Lentils (Green)	High	15-20 minutes	N/A
Lentils (Red)	High	15-17 minutes	N/A
Lima Beans	High	20-24 minutes	10-15 minutes
Navy Beans	High	25-30 minutes	20-25 minutes
Pinto Beans	High	25-30 minutes	20-25 minutes
Red Beans	High	25-30 minutes	20-25 minutes
Soybeans	High	25-30 minutes	20-25 minutes
Split Peas (Green)	High	15-20 minutes	10-15 minutes
Split Peas (Yellow)	High	15-20 minutes	10-15 minutes

Pressure Cooking Meat and Poultry

To achieve best results when cooking meat/poultry, please refer to these tips and hints:

1. Cut meat/poultry into pieces of uniform size for even cooking.
2. When mixing meats, cut those that cook more quickly into larger pieces and those that cook more slowly into smaller pieces.
3. Brown meat in small batches; overcrowding the cooker can result in the meat becoming tough and flavorless.

Meat and Poultry	Pressure Setting	Cooking Time
Beef brisket, whole	High	40-50 minutes
Beef cubes	High	18-23 minutes
Beef oxtail	High	40-50 minutes
Beef short ribs	High	35-40 minutes
Chicken strips, boneless	High	10-12 minutes
Chicken breast	High	8-10 minutes
Chicken cubes	High	10-12 minutes
Chicken legs	High	10-12 minutes
Chicken wings	High	10-12 minutes
Chicken, whole	High	20-25 minutes
Corish Hen	High	10-15 minutes
Duck, whole	High	25-30 minutes
Ham, uncooked	High	26-30 minutes
Lamb, cubes	High	10-13 minutes
Pork spareribs	High	20-25 minutes
Pork chops	High	8-10 minutes
Pork baby back ribs	High	19-24 minutes
Pork loin	High	45-50 minutes
Pork shoulder	High	45-50 minutes
Turkey, drumsticks	High	15-20 minutes
Veal chops	High	5-8 minutes

Pressure Cooking Seafood

To achieve best results when cooking seafood, please refer to these tips and hints:

1. Always leave at least 2 inches from the top rim to prevent overflowing.
2. Smaller types of seafood, such as clams and shrimp, do not take long to cook; therefore, it's best to add these types of seafood to a recipe during the last few minutes of cooking.

Seafood	Pressure Setting	Fresh (Cooking Time)	Frozen (Cooking Time)
Fish, whole	Low	5–6 minutes	7–10 minutes
Fish fillet	Low	2–3 minutes	3–4 minutes
Fish steak	Low	3–4 minutes	4–6 minutes
Crab legs	Low	3–4 minutes	5–6 minutes
Lobster tail	Low	2–3 minutes	3–4 minutes
Lobster, whole	Low	3–4 minutes	4–6 minutes
Mussels	Low	2–3 minutes	4–5 minutes
Scallops, small	Low	1 minute	2 minutes
Scallops, large	Low	2 minutes	3 minutes
Shrimp, with shell	Low	2–3 minutes	3–4 minutes
Shrimp, medium–large	Low	1–2 minutes	2–3 minutes
Shrimp, jumbo	Low	2–3 minutes	3–4 minutes

Pressure Cooking Rice and Grains

To achieve best results when pressure cooking rice/grains, please refer to these tips and hints:

1. Add 1-2 tablespoons of oil to the dried grains to minimize frothing.
2. Do not fill removable cooking pot more than halfway to allow rice/grains to expand in size.
3. Use the natural release method. Do not use the quick release method to release pressure.
4. Pearl barley tends to froth, foam, and sputter, which may block the pressure valve if filled too high in the removable cooking pot. Please be sure to not fill the removable cooking pot more than halfway.
5. Use a high pressure setting for cooking rice and grains.

Rice and Grains	Grain: Water Ratio (180 ml cups)	Cooking Function, Cooking Time
Arborio	1:3	Risotto, 6 minutes
Barley	1:3-1:4	Brown Rice, 25-30 minutes
Basmati	1:1½	White Rice, 6-9 minutes
Brown	1:1¼	Brown Rice, 25-30 minutes
Couscous	1:2	Brown Rice, 5-8 minutes
Jasmine	1:1	White Rice, 8-9 minutes
Long-Grain Rice	1:1½	White Rice, 10 minutes
Millet	2:3	Brown Rice, 10-12 minutes
Pearl Barley	1:4	Risotto, 25-30 minutes
Quick-Cooking Oats	1:1⅔	Risotto, 5-6 minutes
Quinoa	1:2	Brown Rice, 8-10 minutes
Short-Grain Rice	1:1½	White Rice, 8-9 minutes
Steel Cut Oats	1:1⅔	Risotto, 10 minutes
Sushi Rice	1:1½	White Rice, 9 minutes
Wheat Berries	1:3	Brown Rice, 25-30 minutes
Wild Rice	1:3	Brown Rice, 25-30 minutes

RICE COOKING PROGRAMS

(These guidelines are provided courtesy of Fagor America.)

White Rice

Cook rice to perfection every time with the WHITE RICE function. This function is programmable to ensure rice is soft and composed of just the right cooking temperatures. Rice will be fluffy and delicious while eliminating any cooking hassle.

1. Place the removable cooking pot into the multi-cooker.
2. Place about 1–2 tablespoons of oil into the removable cooking pot.
3. Add the water and rice, according to the ratios provided in the chart, and any other desired ingredients into the removable cooking pot.
4. Close and lock the lid of the multi-cooker by properly aligning the handles and turning the lid counterclockwise. Set pressure regulator knob to PRESSURE.
5. Press the WHITE RICE function, which will show a preset time of 10 minutes. If you need to adjust the time, press the + or – buttons to adjust timing and then press the START/STOP button once to begin cooking.
6. As the pressure is building, the WHITE RICE function will blink. Once pressure has been reached, the light will turn solid red, and the unit will beep. This is when your cook time begins and the multi-cooker will start counting down by minutes on the cooker's digital screen.
7. Once cook time is over, the multi-cooker will automatically go to KEEP WARM function until you press the START/STOP button to cancel the program.

Brown Rice

The BROWN RICE function ensures your rice is cooked entirely while maintaining all of its richness and nutrients. This function transforms your rice flawlessly by utilizing a specialized cooking cycle.

1. Place the removable cooking pot into the multi-cooker.
2. Place about 1–2 tablespoons of oil into the removable cooking pot.
3. Add the water and rice, according to the ratios provided in the chart, and any other desired ingredients into the removable cooking pot.
4. Close and lock the lid of the multi-cooker by properly aligning the handles and turning the lid counterclockwise. Set pressure regulator knob to PRESSURE.
5. Press the BROWN RICE function, which will show a preset time of 20 minutes. If you need to adjust the time, press the + or – buttons to adjust timing and then press the START/STOP button once to begin building pressure.

6. As the pressure is building, the BROWN RICE function will blink. Once pressure has been reached, the indicator light will turn solid red, and the unit will beep. This is when your cook time begins and the multi-cooker will start counting down by minutes on the cooker's digital screen.
7. Once cook time is over, the multi-cooker will automatically go to KEEP WARM function until you press the START/STOP button to cancel the program.

Risotto

The RISOTTO function ensures the temperature is perfectly precise. Create risotto that has the perfect blend of timing, temperature, and taste!

1. Place the removable cooking pot into the multi-cooker.
2. Place about 1 tablespoon of vegetable or olive oil into the removable cooking pot and choose SAUTÉ function to sauté the Arborio rice and other ingredients for about 1–2 minutes. Keep the lid off while sautéing.
3. Add water or stock and any seasoning or ingredients needed. Once the liquid comes to a rapid boil, properly close and lock the pressure cooker lid.
4. Choose the RISOTTO function, which will be preset to 6 minutes. If you need to adjust the time for the recipe, press the + or – buttons to do so.
5. Press the START/STOP button once to begin building pressure. The RISOTTO function will blink as its building pressure.
6. Once pressure has been built, the red blinking light on the RISOTTO function will go solid red, and the unit will beep. This is when your cook time begins and the multi-cooker will start counting down by minutes on the cooker's digital screen.
7. After your cooking time is over, the multi-cooker will automatically switch to the KEEP WARM function until you press the START/STOP button to cancel the program.

CONVERSION CHARTS

METRIC AND IMPERIAL CONVERSIONS
(These conversions are rounded for convenience)

Ingredient	Cups/Tablespoons/Teaspoons	Ounces	Grams/Milliliters
Butter	1 cup/ 16 tablespoons/ 2 sticks	8 ounces	230 grams
Cheese, shredded	1 cup	4 ounces	110 grams
Cream cheese	1 tablespoon	0.5 ounce	14.5 grams
Cornstarch	1 tablespoon	0.3 ounce	8 grams
Flour, all-purpose	1 cup/1 tablespoon	4.5 ounces/0.3 ounce	125 grams/8 grams
Flour, whole wheat	1 cup	4 ounces	120 grams
Fruit, dried	1 cup	4 ounces	120 grams
Fruits or veggies, chopped	1 cup	5 to 7 ounces	145 to 200 grams
Fruits or veggies, puréed	1 cup	8.5 ounces	245 grams
Honey, maple syrup, or corn syrup	1 tablespoon	.75 ounce	20 grams
Liquids: cream, milk, water, or juice	1 cup	8 fluid ounces	240 milliliters
Oats	1 cup	5.5 ounces	150 grams
Salt	1 teaspoon	0.2 ounces	6 grams
Spices: cinnamon, cloves, ginger, or nutmeg (ground)	1 teaspoon	0.2 ounce	5 milliliters
Sugar, brown, firmly packed	1 cup	7 ounces	200 grams
Sugar, white	1 cup/1 tablespoon	7 ounces/0.5 ounce	200 grams/12.5 grams
Vanilla extract	1 teaspoon	0.2 ounce	4 grams

OVEN TEMPERATURES

Fahrenheit	Celsius	Gas Mark
225°	110°	¼
250°	120°	½
275°	140°	1
300°	150°	2
325°	160°	3
350°	180°	4
375°	190°	5
400°	200°	6
425°	220°	7
450°	230°	8

INDEX

CONNECT AND SHARE WITH US!

Cami

Instagram: camitidbits
Facebook: camitidbits
Pinterest: tidbitscami
Twitter: camitidbits

Marci

Instagram: marcitidbits
Facebook: marcitidbits
Pinterest: marcitidbits
Twitter: marcitidbits

For more recipes and to follow us along on our blogging adventures, visit **www.tidbits-marci.com** or **www.tidbits-cami.com**

Share your recipe results with us by tagging us on social media and using the hashtag **#mastertheelectricpressurecooker**

To ask questions, share recipes, results, or ideas, and connect with a community of pressure cooker enthusiasts, request access to our "Master the Electric Pressure Cooker" Facebook group: **https://www.facebook.com/groups/mastertheelectricpressurecooker/**